# AMERICAN HERITAGE

*June, 1971 • Volume XXII, Number 4*

# In Memoriam

ALLAN NEVINS
1890–1971

*DeWitt Clinton Professor of History, Columbia University, 1931–58. Biographer of, among others, Grover Cleveland, Hamilton Fish, John Charles Frémont, John D. Rockefeller, and Henry Ford (with Frank E. Hill). Winner of the Bancroft Prize for history, 1947, for the first two volumes of* Ordeal of the Union. *Twice winner of the Pulitzer Prize for biography, 1933 and 1937. Founder, Oral History Research Office, Columbia University, 1948. Founder, Allan Nevins Chair in American Economic History, Columbia University, 1965. Twice holder of Harmsworth Chair in American History, Oxford University, 1940–41 and 1964–65. President, Society of American Historians, 1946–61, one of the sponsoring groups of* AMERICAN HERITAGE. *President, American Historical Association, 1959. President, American Academy of Arts and Letters, 1966–68. Chairman of the Editorial Advisory Board of* AMERICAN HERITAGE *magazine, 1954–71.*

They say a tree is best measured when it is down. Allan Nevins is gone, at last, although he seemed imperishable, and we at AMERICAN HERITAGE feel a poignant sense of loss. We measure him now by the length of the shadow he cast, and by the abiding influence he had upon us and upon the magazine we serve. We also think of the friendship which he extended to everyone who knew him, and that is immeasurable.

A good many different men had a part in the founding of this magazine, but it seems safe to say that it would not exist in its present form but for the influence of Allan Nevins. Nevins was one of the great American historians, and perhaps he was greatest of all in this: he wrote history, not simply as a means of talking with other historians, but in order to talk to the general reader. He was in the grand tradition of Francis Parkman and William H. Prescott, which is to say that he was a skilled literary craftsman; and he was firmly convinced that history, written down and put between covers, has to be much more than a collection of Ph.D. theses. It has to give its reader a sense of the drama, the subtle excitement, and the immediacy of the events in his nation's past. If it cannot give this, it fails; if it does give it, it enriches the life and broadens the horizon of the person who reads it.

How well or how inadequately this magazine may have embodied this ideal is perhaps a separate question. The point is that this was the vision Allan Nevins had, and this was the ideal that he kept insisting we should assimilate. He saw history as something exciting and moving as well as instructive; the people of the past were people of the present day, with both the faults and the virtues that we present-day folk see all about us; what they did shapes our own lives, and to follow them is to learn more than we can otherwise know about the values by which human life is lived and by which, at times, it has to be surrendered.

We used to have a way, on the staff of this magazine, of referring to Allan Nevins affectionately as our Faculty Adviser. This was all very well, in a sense, and at times there was something vaguely remindful of a staff of undergraduates engaged in a publishing venture, with a helpful professor standing by to ward off untimely errors. (This of course harks back to the long-gone day when students would allow a faculty adviser to come on the premises at all.) But the parallel is imperfect. My own experience in such matters, dating back (as it seems now) to the Neo-Pleistocene age, is that the faculty adviser was there chiefly to tell us what we could not do. As one of the guiding spirits of AMERICAN HERITAGE, Allan put the emphasis on what we ought to do. He had command of few negatives. He could see only the rich field of American history and the way in which its separate chapters could best be described. In the matter of calling these chapters to our attention and helping to find the persons best qualified to describe them, he was something of a genius.

That word *genius* is sometimes misapplied. It has been described, imperfectly, as a capacity for taking infinite pains, and that capacity Allan Nevins assuredly had. But anyone who worked with him was bound to broaden the definition a little. Genius, as Nevins displayed it, was at least partly a matter of having and using boundless energy.

He was one of the busiest of living men, but he was never too busy to give help to someone else. If you had a problem, you could lay it in front of him, certain that he would give it as much time as you needed, certain also that in the end he would strike a light to illumine the path you had to follow. To be sure, the moment he felt that he had done all he could do for you, he became very busy again. He had no time to spare; he would jump up, slip into his coat before you quite realized that the consultation was over, and go out of there, coattails adrift in the breeze. He was all yours as long as you needed him, but he had no time for small talk.

It would of course be an error to assume that this man's impact on American historiography came simply because he insisted that history must be well written. He was equally concerned with the collection of it—with the hard spadework that has to precede the moment when the historian puts paper into typewriter and starts to produce manuscript. He knew where the papers were, he went and looked at them and made copious notes—and probably it should be mentioned that his knowledge and even his notes were at the service of any budding historian who was following in his steps. He not only knew where the papers were; he saw to it that papers which would not otherwise have existed came into being, and one of his great services was to establish the Oral History Project at Columbia University—an operation whereby men who had played a part in the making of history were persuaded to dictate into a tape recorder what they knew about great events, so that students in some future generation could have access to knowledge that would otherwise have vanished forever.

But simply to list the contributions Allan Nevins made does not seem like enough. Everyone who knew him knew that to touch him was to touch greatness: greatness not only of mind and professional achievements, but also of heart and soul. No one could work with him without being richer for it. If we who work on AMERICAN HERITAGE feel a deep sense of loss in his passing, it is not solely because he did so much for this magazine. It is because he did so much for us as individual human beings.

—*Bruce Catton*

*When I am grown to man's estate*
*I shall be very proud and great*
*And tell the other girls and boys*
*Not to meddle with my toys.*

—Robert Louis Stevenson,
*A Child's Garden of Verses*

WHOM DID THEY GROW UP TO BE? SEE OPPOSITE PAGE.

# AMERICAN HERITAGE

*The Magazine of History*

SENIOR EDITOR
Bruce Catton

EDITOR
Oliver Jensen

ARTICLES EDITOR
E. M. Halliday

EXECUTIVE EDITOR
Nat Brandt

ASSOCIATE EDITORS
Barbara Klaw          Bernard A. Weisberger

ART DIRECTOR
Emma Landau

PICTURE EDITORS
Carla Davidson          Mary Dawn Earley

COPY EDITOR
Joyce O'Connor
ASSISTANT: Devorah Kanter

ASSISTANT TO THE EDITOR
Ekaterina L. Trofimov

CONSULTING EDITOR: Joan Paterson Kerr

CONTRIBUTING EDITOR: Robert C. Alberts

ADVISORY BOARD
Allan Nevins, *Chairman*
(1954–1971)

Carl Carmer                 Louis C. Jones
Gerald Carson               Alvin M. Josephy, Jr.
Marshall B. Davidson        Howard H. Peckham
John A. Garraty             Francis S. Ronalds
Eric F. Goldman             S. K. Stevens

AMERICAN HERITAGE PUBLISHING CO., INC.

PRESIDENT AND PUBLISHER
Paul Gottlieb

EDITOR IN CHIEF
Joseph J. Thorndike

SENIOR EDITOR
Richard M. Ketchum

EDITORIAL ART DIRECTOR
Murray Belsky

AMERICAN HERITAGE is published every two months by American Heritage Publishing Co., Inc.; editorial and executive offices, 551 Fifth Avenue, New York, N.Y. 10017. Treasurer, Marjorie C. Dyer; Secretary, John C. Taylor III. Correspondence about subscriptions should be sent to American Heritage Subscription Office, 383 West Center Street, Marion, Ohio 43302. Single copies: $5.00. Annual subscriptions: $20.00 in U.S. and Canada; $21.00 elsewhere.

A ten-year Index covering Volumes VI–XV is available at $5.00; a new five-year Index of Volumes XVI–XX has just been published at $3.50.

AMERICAN HERITAGE will consider but assumes no responsibility for unsolicited materials. Title registered U.S. Patent Office. Second-class postage paid at New York, N.Y., and at additional mailing offices.

Sponsored by
*American Association for State & Local History · Society of American Historians*

CONTENTS *June, 1971 · Volume XXII, Number 4*

IN MEMORIAM: ALLAN NEVINS . . . . . . . . 2

ENGLAND'S VIETNAM: THE AMERICAN REVOLUTION
*by Richard M. Ketchum* . . . . . . . . 6

WHICH WAY, AMERICA? DULLES ALWAYS KNEW
*by R. D. Challener with John Fenton* . . . . . . 12

SPOON RIVER REVISITED
*by Edward Laning, with illustrations by the author* . . . . 14

SWEET EXTRACT OF HOKUM   *by Gerald Carson* . . . . 18

ECHOES OF THE LITTLE BIGHORN
*Portraits and text by David Humphreys Miller* . . . . 28
EPILOGUE: Twenty years after . . . *by Robert M. Utley* . . . 40

PICNICS LONG AGO . . . . . . . . . 42

SPHAIRISTIKÉ, ANYONE?   *by E. M. Halliday* . . . . . 48

HELL'S HIGHWAY TO ARNHEM   *by Stephen W. Sears* . . 60

A MAN, A PLAN, A CANAL, PANAMA!   *by David G. McCullough* . . 64

TO THE FLAG   *by Nat Brandt* . . . . . . . 72

THE UNTOLD DELIGHTS OF DULUTH . . . . . 76

POSTSCRIPTS TO HISTORY . . . . . . . 111

THE REVISIONIST: LEXINGTON, 1775
*Drawn by Michael Ramus* . . . . . . . . 112

COVER: Joseph High Eagle was a young Oglala Sioux warrior of sixteen in the summer of 1876 when "Long Hair," Lt. Col. George A. Custer, attacked the great Indian encampment on the Little Bighorn River; he fought in this last great Indian battle under his cousin, Crazy Horse, until all of the five companies under the impetuous hero were wiped out. In his old age he posed in his war bonnet for the writer and artist David Humphreys Miller, who in 1935 began collecting the reminiscences and portraits of Indians then still surviving that fight. Four of these previously unpublished memoirs commence on page 36. All the warriors have gone to the happy hunting ground since then, including High Eagle, killed by a careless white motorist while, at the side of a road, aged ninety, he stood answering Nature's imperious call. BACK COVER: This trade card is from the collection of Mr. and Mrs. Albert E. Castel, Jr., of Wichita. For more on patent medicines see Gerald Carson's article on page 18. FRONTISPIECE: All boys, they are Presidents Taft (top left) and Franklin Roosevelt (bottom), and John Foster Dulles, subject of an article beginning on page 12.

FRONTISPIECE CREDITS: CINCINNATI HISTORICAL SOCIETY; FRANKLIN D. ROOSEVELT LIBRARY; JOHN FOSTER DULLES PAPERS, PRINCETON UNIVERSITY LIBRARY

*A domino theory, distant wilderness warfare, the notion of
"defensive enclaves," hawks, doves, hired mercenaries, possible
intervention by hostile powers, a little trouble telling friendly natives
from unfriendly—George III went through the whole routine*

# England's Vietnam:
# THE AMERICAN REVOLUTION

*By* RICHARD M. KETCHUM

If it is true that those who cannot remember the past are condemned to repeat it, America's last three Presidents might have profited by examining the ghostly footsteps of America's last king before pursuing their adventure in Vietnam. As the United States concludes a decade of war in Southeast Asia, it is worth recalling the time, two centuries ago, when Britain faced the same agonizing problems in America that we have met in Vietnam. History seldom repeats itself exactly, and it would be a mistake to try to equate the ideologies or the motivating factors involved; but enough disturbing parallels may be drawn between those two distant events to make one wonder if the Messrs. Kennedy, Johnson, and Nixon had their ears closed while the class was studying the American Revolution.

Britain, on the eve of that war, was the greatest empire since Rome. Never before had she known such wealth and power; never had the future seemed so bright, the prospects so glowing. All, that is, except the spreading sore of discontent in the American colonies that, after festering for a decade and more, finally erupted in violence at Lexington and Concord on April 19, 1775. When news of the subsequent battle for Bunker Hill reached England that summer, George III and his ministers concluded that there was no alternative to using force to put down the insurrection. In the King's mind, at least, there was no longer any hope of reconciliation—nor did the idea appeal to him. He was determined to teach the rebellious colonials a lesson, and no doubts troubled him as to the righteousness of the course he had chosen. "I am not sorry that the line of conduct seems now chalked out," he had said even before fighting began; later he told his prime minister, Lord North, "I know

Frederick, Lord North, whom
Charles James Fox called "the blundering
pilot who had brought the nation into
its present difficulties," believed,
as did his sovereign, George III, that
"blows must decide" whether the Americans
would be subject to the laws of
Great Britain or independent.

I am doing my Duty and I can never wish to retract." And then, making acceptance of the war a matter of personal loyalty, "I wish nothing but good," he said, "therefore anyone who does not agree with me is a traitor and a scoundrel." Filled with high moral purpose and confidence, he was certain that "when once these rebels have felt a smart blow, they will submit . . ."

In British political and military circles there was general agreement that the war would be quickly and easily won. "Shall we be told," asked one of the King's men in Commons, "that [the Americans] can resist the powerful efforts of this nation?" Major John Pitcairn, writing home from Boston in March, 1775, said, "I am satisfied that one active campaign, a smart action, and burning two or three of their towns, will set everything to rights." The man who would direct the British navy during seven years of war, the unprincipled, inefficient Earl of Sandwich, rose in the House of Lords to express his opinion of the provincial fighting man. "Suppose the Colonies do abound in men," the First Lord of the Admiralty asked, "what does that signify? They are raw, undisciplined, cowardly men. I wish instead of forty or fifty thousand of these *brave* fellows they would produce in the field at least two hundred thousand; the more the better, the easier would be the conquest; if they did not run away, they would starve themselves into compliance with our measures. . . ." And General James Murray, who had succeeded the great Wolfe in 1749 as commander in North America, called the native American "a very effeminate thing, very unfit for and very impatient of war." Between these estimates of the colonial militiaman and a belief that the might of Great Britain was invincible, there was a kind of arrogant optimism in official quarters when the conflict began. "As there is not common sense in protracting a war of this sort," wrote Lord George Germain, the secretary for the American colonies, in September, 1775, "I should be for exerting the utmost force of this Kingdom to finish the rebellion in one campaign."

Optimism bred more optimism, arrogance more arrogance. One armchair strategist in the House of Commons, William Innes, outlined for the other members an elaborate scheme he had devised for the conduct of the war. First, he would remove the British troops from Boston, since that place was poorly situated for defense. Then, while the people of the Massachusetts Bay Colony were treated like the madmen they were and shut up by the navy, the army would move to one of the southern colonies, fortify itself in an impregnable position, and let the provincials attack if they pleased. The British could sally forth from this and other defensive enclaves at will, and eventually "success against one-half of America will pave the way to the conquest of the whole. . . ." What was more, Innes went on, it was "more than probable you may find men to recruit your army in America." There was a good possibility, in other words, that the British regulars would be replaced after a while by Americans who were loyal to their king, so that the army fighting the rebels would be Americanized, so to speak, and the Irish and English lads sent home. General James Robertson also believed that success lay in this scheme of Americanizing the combat force: "I never had an idea of subduing the Americans," he said, "I meant to assist the good Americans to subdue the bad."

This notion was important not only from the standpoint of the fighting, but in terms of administering the colonies once they were beaten; loyalists would take over the reins of government when the British pulled out, and loyalist militiamen would preserve order in the pacified colonies. No one knew, of course, how many "good" Americans there were; some thought they might make up half or more of the population. Shortly after arriving in the colonies in 1775, General William Howe, for one, was convinced that "the insurgents are very few, in comparison with the whole of the people."

Before taking the final steps into full-scale war, however, the King and his ministers had to be certain about one vitally important matter: they had to be able to count on the support of the English people. On several occasions in 1775 they were able to read the public pulse (that part of it, at least, that mattered) by observing certain important votes in Parliament. The King's address to both Houses on October 26, in which he announced plans to suppress the uprising in America, was followed by weeks of angry debate; but when the votes were counted, the North ministry's majority was overwhelming. Each vote indicated the full tide of anger that influenced the independent members, the country gentlemen who agreed that the colonials must be put in their place and taught a lesson. A bit out of touch with the news, highly principled, and content in the belief that the King and the ministry must be right, none of them seem to have asked what would be best for the empire; they simply went along with the vindictive measures that were being set in motion. Eloquent voices—those of Edmund Burke, Charles James Fox, the Earl of Chatham, John Wilkes, among others—were raised in opposition to the policies of the Crown, but as Burke said, ". . . it was almost in vain to contend, for the country gentlemen had abandoned their duty, and placed an implicit confidence in the Minister."

The words of sanity and moderation went unheeded because the men who spoke them were out of power and out of public favor; and each time the votes were tallied, the strong, silent, unquestioning majority prevailed. No one in any position of power in the government proposed, after the Battle of Bunker Hill, to halt the fighting in order to settle the differences; no one seriously contemplated conversations that might have led to peace. Instead the government— like so many governments before and since—took what appeared to be the easy way out and settled for war.

George III was determined to maintain his empire, intact and undiminished, and his greatest fear was that the loss of the American colonies would set off a reaction like a line of dominoes falling. Writing to Lord North in 1779, he called the contest with America "the most serious in which any country was ever engaged. It contains

"A great empire and little minds
go ill together," declared Edmund Burke
in his speech "On Conciliation with America."
"The proposition is peace,"
Burke reminded the Commons. "It is peace
sought in the spirit of peace . . ." But
despite his eloquence and logic, his
proposal was voted down, 271 to 78.
THE BRITISH MUSEUM

9

"Beg your pardon," says this armchair
strategist of 1779, "had it from
my Lord Fiddle Faddle. He'd nothing to do
but cut 'em off, pass the Susquehanna and
proceed to Boston, possess himself of
Crown Point—then Philadelphia would have
fallen of course and a communication
open'd with the Northern Army—
as easily as I'd open a vein."

such a train of consequences that they must be examined to feel its real weight. . . . Independence is [the Americans'] object, which every man not willing to sacrifice every object to a momentary and inglorious peace must concur with me in thinking this country can never submit to. Should America succeed in that, the West Indies must follow, not in independence, but for their own interest they must become dependent on America. Ireland would soon follow, and this island reduced to itself, would be a poor island indeed."

Despite George's unalterable determination, strengthened by his domino theory; despite the wealth and might of the British empire; despite all the odds favoring a quick triumph, the problems facing the King and his ministers and the armed forces were formidable ones indeed. Surpassing all others in sheer magnitude was the immense distance between the mother country and the rebellious colonies. As Edmund Burke described the situation in his last, most eloquent appeal for conciliation, "Three thousand miles of ocean lie between you and them. No contrivance can prevent the effect of this distance in weakening government. Seas roll, and months pass, between the order and the execution; and the want of a speedy explanation of a single point is enough to defeat a whole system." Often the westerly passage took three months, and every soldier, every weapon, every button and gaiter and musket ball, every article of clothing and great quantities of food and even fuel, had to be shipped across those three thousand miles of the Atlantic. It was not only immensely costly and time consuming, but there was a terrifying wastefulness to it. Ships sank or were blown hundreds of miles off course, supplies spoiled, animals died en route. Worse yet, men died, and in substantial numbers: returns from regiments sent from the British Isles to the West Indies between 1776 and 1780 reveal that an average of 11 per cent of the troops was lost on these crossings.

Beyond the water lay the North American land mass, and it was an article of faith on the part of many a British military man that certain ruin lay in fighting an enemy on any large scale in that savage wilderness. In the House of Lords in November, 1775, the Duke of Richmond warned the peers to consult their geographies before turning their backs on a peaceful settlement. There was, he said, "one insuperable difficulty with which an army would have to struggle"—America abounded in vast rivers that provided natural barriers to the progress of troops; it was a country in which every bush might conceal an enemy, a land whose cultivated parts would be laid waste, so that "the army (if any army could march or subsist) would be obliged to draw all its provisions from Europe, and all its fresh meat from Smithfield market." The French, the mortal enemies of Great Britain, who had seen a good deal more of the North American wilds than the English had, were already laying plans to capitalize on the situation when the British army was bogged down there. In Paris, watchfully eyeing his adversary's every move, France's foreign minister, the Comte de Vergennes, predicted in July, 1775, that "it will be vain for the English to multiply their forces" in the colonies; "no longer can they bring that vast continent back to dependence by force of arms." Seven years later, as the war drew to a close, one of Rochambeau's aides told a friend of Charles James Fox: "No opinion was clearer than that though the people of America might be conquered by well disciplined European troops, the country of America was unconquerable."

Yet even in 1775 some thoughtful Englishmen doubted if the American people or their army could be defeated. Before the news of Bunker Hill arrived in London, the adjutant general declared that a plan to defeat the colonials militarily was "as wild an idea as ever controverted common sense," and the secretary-at-war, Lord Barrington, had similar reservations. As early as 1774 Barrington ventured the opinion that a war in the wilderness of North America would cost Britain far more than she could ever gain from it; that the size of the country and the colonials' familiarity with firearms would make victory questionable—or at best achievable only at the cost of enormous suffering; and finally, even if Britain should win such a contest, Barrington believed that the cost of maintaining the colonies in any state of subjection would be staggering. John Wilkes, taunting Lord North on this matter of military conquest, suggested that North—even if he rode out at the head of the entire English cavalry—would not venture ten miles into the countryside for fear of guerrilla fighters. "The Americans," Wilkes promised, "will dispute every inch of territory with you, every narrow pass, every strong defile, every Thermopylae, every Bunker's Hill."

It was left to the great William Pitt to provide the most stirring warning against fighting the Americans. Now Earl of Chatham, he was so crippled in mind and body that he rarely appeared in the House of Lords, but in May, 1777, he made the supreme effort, determined to raise his voice once again in behalf of conciliation. Supported on canes, his eyes flashing with the old fire and his beak-like face thrust forward belligerently, he warned the peers: "You cannot conquer the Americans. You talk of your numerous friends to annihilate the Congress, and of your powerful forces to disperse their army, but I might as well talk of driving them before me with this crutch. . . . You have been three years teaching them the art of war, and they are apt scholars. I will venture to tell your lordships that the American gentry will make officers enough fit to command the troops of all the European powers. What you have sent there are too many to make peace, too few to make war. You cannot make them respect you. You cannot make them wear your cloth. You will plant an invincible hatred in their breast against you . . ."

"My lords," he went on, "you have been the aggressors from the beginning. I say again, this country has been the aggressor. You have made descents upon their coasts. You have burnt their towns, plundered their country, made war upon the inhabitants, confiscated their property, proscribed and imprisoned their persons. . . . The people of America look upon Parliament as the authors of their miseries. Their affections are estranged from their sovereign. Let, then, reparation come from the hands that inflicted the injuries. Let

CONTINUED ON PAGE 81

After Lexington, Captain W. G. Evelyn of the "King's Own" Regiment said the Americans, caricatured here, "are the most absolute cowards on the face of the earth, yet they are just now worked up to such a degree of enthusiasm and madness that they are easily persuaded the Lord is to assist them . . . and that they must be invincible."

THE METROPOLITAN MUSEUM OF ART

11

*The job ran in the family; both his uncle and grandfather
were Secretaries of State. Home life in a parsonage taught him piety,
and the law precision. The rigid views of a world divided
between good and evil he worked out, apparently, himself. Private letters and
new taped recollections help explain the shaping of the man
who set our Cold War foreign policy*

# Which Way America?
## DULLES ALWAYS KNEW

*By* R. D. CHALLENER *with* JOHN FENTON

About a dozen years ago Carol Burnett's nightclub repertoire included a number, "I Made
a Fool of Myself over John Foster Dulles." In 1971, in an era of massive discontent with
American foreign policy, Miss Burnett would be unwise to restore it to her program. For
even though the song is pure camp, some youthful member of her audience would certainly
jump to his feet with a denunciation of Dulles as the archetypal villain of the foreign-policy
establishment he repudiates. To the new generation Foster Dulles stands condemned as the
very model of the Modern Cold Warrior. To them he is the moralist whose platitudes reduced the world situation to a struggle between Western "good" and Communist "evil" and
the brinkman who stood poised on the edge of Armageddon and revelled in the confrontation. His veto of United States assistance in the building of Egypt's Aswan Dam, the indict-
ment further runs, alienated Gamal Abdel Nasser and began the fatal series of steps that led
to a massive Soviet influence in the Middle East, against which we are now contending. At
the real brink, some of his other critics assert, he frustrated the Anglo-French-Israeli armed
intervention at Suez, without providing any countermeasure to preserve the Western position in that area. Finally, it is charged, his efforts to maintain staunch anti-Communist
leadership in power in Saigon after 1954 make the Vietnam war in good part his legacy.

John Foster Dulles dominated American foreign policy during the more than six years
that he was Secretary of State, and was always a controversial figure. In his speeches, especially those that were televised, he presented the image of a one-dimensional man, the stern
Presbyterian whose stock in trade was an unbending stance against "atheistic communism"

CONTINUED ON PAGE 84

*Stabbing the air with a minatory forefinger, John Foster Dulles, in a press
conference, displays his best evangelistic stance. To the vexation of his foes
and the admiration of friends, Dulles—described as a "card-carrying Christian"—exuded a sense of moral certainty that shadowed his human side.*
U.P.I.

13

I always felt at home in Edgar Lee Masters' quarters in the Chelsea Hotel. It was all so much like a Petersburg, Illinois, law office that I might have been back in Papa Smoot's office overlooking the courthouse square. Edgar Lee, plain and short and stocky, sat in a straight chair near a big desk. There was the same smell of books and tobacco. The same southern light filtered through the branches of the ailanthus trees, and the court behind the Chelsea was almost as quiet as the empty Petersburg square with its big elms. There was even a spittoon on the floor near Masters' chair.

I had never known Edgar Lee in Petersburg. When I was growing up there, he lived in Chicago, where he practiced law, and after the shock of *Spoon River Anthology* he was no longer welcome in his home town. Too many of the characters in the book were recognizable in spite of the made-up names attached to them. In later years he could only return secretly because there was some sort of court order against him in a matter of alimony. And anyway, if I had talked to him, Papa Smoot would have been furious when he found out (and everybody in town knew everything about everybody).

It was through Miss Edith, Edgar Lee's cousin and my high school history teacher, that I came to know and revere the poet. Edgar Lee was a secret cult of Miss Edith's, but one she chose to share with me. She would read to me sometimes from his letters and from poems he sent to her. (*"A Corybantic din, as of a Salvation Army, followed Him. . . . And then along came Paul who almost spoiled it all."*) I have always thought that Edgar Lee might have written "Emily Sparks" with Miss Edith in mind. (And inevitably I became Reuben Pantier. "Dear Emily Sparks"! Dear Miss Edith!) I don't remember if I ever betrayed these great confidences at home. If I did, Mama and Papa Smoot would have put it down to Miss Edith's spinsterish eccentricity. All Edgar Lee ever said to me of her was that she had wasted her life caring for her mother and father.

He always seemed glad to see me, and I think he enjoyed my visits, because he loved Petersburg and it was of Petersburg that we talked. I believe that the Petersburg of long ago was more real to him than the great city outside the Chelsea Hotel. I was proud of the fact that he had mentioned me in his book about the Sangamon, the river that flows past New Salem and Petersburg, but I had an uneasy feeling that it was my origins he was interested in and that it was not I he was seeing but my Grandfather Laning's house, "all of pressed brick and Victorian towers and balconies, standing in picturesque view at the foot of the hill which one passes going out of town toward Tallula." He seemed to me to be lonely and sad and to be living in the days of his youth. Sometimes, though, my visits were interrupted by the appearance of a pretty young woman who lived upstairs and who took a

*By* EDWARD LANING

ILLUSTRATIONS BY THE AUTHOR

14

# Spoon River Revisited

*An artist recalls his Midwestern home town and the poet who made it famous*

The Schirding farm: "*It was June. . . . The deep grass of the pasture rippled like waves in the fragrant west wind*" proprietary interest in him that visibly brightened his day. She would come in smiling to fuss about his health and to tell him, "I think I've found a first edition; I'll know for sure tomorrow," and she would leave me wondering whether, except for my being there, she might not have stayed. And this was not like Papa Smoot's office.

When she had gone, we were back in Petersburg. Edgar Lee would light a cigar, lean back comfortably in his chair, and look out at the ailanthus trees. "The old Courthouse America is dead," I would hear him say. "The old Jeffersonian democracy is gone. The beginning of the end was the rise of the Republican Party after the Civil War." Then he would launch into a tirade against Roosevelt and the New Deal. When I left him to walk back to the pier in the Hudson River where I was painting Prometheus for the ceiling of the New York Public Library, a New Deal project, I felt annoyed with him. He was in his seventies, I in my thirties, and life in the present seemed glorious to me.

Several years after Papa Smoot's death I went back to Petersburg to paint a picture of the old farmhouse on the Schirding place north of town. I walked from the house past a barnyard where John Schirding kept some fine horses, including a great white stallion, and then along a fence behind which a fat grunting sow was suckling her squealing pigs and into a pasture where I set up my easel. It was June and the countryside was verdant. The deep grass of the pasture rippled like waves in the fragrant west wind. There were sparrows and meadowlarks in the bright air, and butterflies, and in the grass there were beetles and field mice and sometimes a green snake.

The old Schirding place was not far from the top of the long grade where the C. P. & St.L. chugged slowly up from the Sangamon Valley to the high prairie that

Grandfather Laning: "*. . . the house I built on the hill, With its spires, bay windows, and roof of slate*"

stretched away as level as the sea to a far horizon. In the late afternoon I would hear the freight train's steam engine puffing hard to make the grade and then see it appear over the top, where it seemed to sigh with relief and go rattling away to the northwest in the direction of the Masters' place at Sandridge, its great spreading plume of smoke red against the late afternoon sky. I thought to myself that I had not realized when I was a child how rich and abundant was the land I grew up in. I had almost forgotten the yellow violets that sprang up in the springtime under layers of last year's leaves in hidden gullies; the little, secret springs of fresh water that flowed away in brooks where crawdaddies hid under the rocks; the beautiful birds that abounded everywhere, orioles and cardinals and bluebirds; the coveys of speckled quail that thrived on the scattered wheat at threshing time; the mourning doves on the telephone lines, their contralto note mingling with the singing of the wires in the wind; the whippoorwill's call in the river-bottom woods where it was cool on summer nights.

I recalled what Edgar Lee had written about his grandfather's farm at Sandridge, where he spent his boyhood:

all with green fields in the spring, golden fields in harvesttime, with sweet smells of the clover blown from afar and from near by the long winds in the June days. So often I walked and raced the four miles from Atterberry to the Masters farmhouse, so eager to get there that I could scarcely contain myself. There was bindweed on the rail fences, horsetails, cattails and pondweeds on the pools of water. There was rich meadow grass, and in season dandelions, milkweed, ironweed, and the purple blossoms of the jimson weed. Around the rim of the landscape seemed to soar the forestry in that clear atmosphere. If I had

Edgar Lee Masters in the Chelsea Hotel: "*so much like Petersburg*"

taken time to loiter in the woods along the way I would have found May apples, wood violets, the flower of Illinois, spring beauties, jack-in-the-pulpit, wake-robin and lady-slippers.

It was from Masters that I learned that in the Potawatomi language *sangamon* means "where there is plenty to eat." And I thought as I stood in the Schirding's pasture that what Edgar Lee and I had in common more deeply than anything else was not people, but the place.

One day at the Chelsea, Masters gave me the typescript of a new poem, "Owen's Bridge," about a rickety crossing of the Sangamon that I remembered, and, as we always did while talking of these things, we had a good time. I said to him, "Lambert Hutchins in *Spoon River* is my Grandfather Laning, isn't he?"

He looked at me with a sly smile and said, "Well, you know, nobody in *Spoon River* is any particular person *exactly.*"

I mentioned my Grandfather Smoot and his disapproval of the poem about Ann Rutledge that had been carved on her tombstone at Oakland Cemetery. "Smoot!" he snorted. "That prig!"

"Papa Smoot is the best man who ever lived," I said. He made a face. "I don't doubt it," he replied.

But Papa Smoot *was* the best man who ever lived. In spite of Edgar Lee Masters, I will always think so. One has to believe in something besides Art. And it was always easy for me to admire him, even as a child. He was the patriarch of a large family, and wherever any of us lived, in one or another of the houses he owned in the town, we always gathered at Papa Smoot's house for Sunday dinner and on holidays. After dinner he would take me for a long walk to the brickyard or the canning factory, and it always made me proud to walk beside him. In the summertime we would go out to the farm at Curtis to see how the wheat was coming along. I often went with him to political rallies at Oakford or Fancy Prairie or Pleasant Plains. Once he took me to Springfield to hear Teddy Roosevelt make a speech at the armory. (I only remember that when Teddy was introduced, he unfastened the velvet rope across the platform, shouted, "Let nothing come between me and the people!" bared his teeth, and the audience went wild.)

Papa and Mama Smoot had always been my second parents, and after my mother died and my father ran away, they were simply Mama and Papa to my sister and me. It was Mama who actually ran things, but her worship for Papa was complete, and she ruled through seductiveness and outward submission. I was their favorite grandson and they spoiled me. It was through Mama that I had my own way. Mama and Papa slept in a big double bed downstairs, and I always knew that if she agreed with me, Papa would wake up agreeing with me in the morning.

Papa Smoot's great goodness hadn't been difficult to achieve; he had always had everything going for him. He had inherited a lot of rich, Illinois farm land; he was intelligent and educated; above all, he was perfectly beautiful. It was no wonder that his goodness was marred by self-righteousness. Petersburg, Illinois, was a very self-righteous community, and Papa was very much a part of Petersburg—in many ways, in fact, its leading citizen. His grandfather had come to Illinois when it was virgin prairie and had acquired a big tract of government land. Abe Lincoln had settled in the locality about the same time and had worked for Papa's grandfather as a hired hand (and borrowed two hundred dollars from him for clothes and travelling expenses to get to Vandalia when he was elected to the legislature). But Lincoln was an ambitious politician, and he moved on to Springfield and

Papa Smoot, looking out his office window at Petersburg's square: "*I wonder if these towns will ever come back.*"

Washington, and Petersburg never liked him very much. The Smoots stayed put and lived comfortably off the fat of the land and were satisfied with themselves.

I always liked to go and sit in Papa Smoot's law office on the courthouse square. When I was a boy, he practiced law in partnership with my father, and the office was a busy place. Papa didn't need to make money from his profession and never tried to. There were endless questions of property rights, and everyone in the county trusted him, and his law practice was an exercise in civic virtue. When now and then someone came to him about a divorce, he would order him out of the office. He didn't believe in divorce. In his last, lonely years, when I would return from New York to visit him, I found him alone there more often than not. His law business had declined

CONTINUED ON PAGE 104

# J. C. HURST & SONS

## STANDARD REMEDIES.

### BRIGHTER HOURS WILL COME.

# PHILADELPHIA, PA.

# SWEET EXTRACT OF HOKUM

Patent medicines were usually neither patented nor medicinal, which is not to say they didn't (and don't) have any effect

ESTABLISHED 1833.

MERCHANTS GARGLING OIL

A LINIMENT FOR MAN & BEAST

If you can identify the period when gentlemen wore genuine ormolu fobs attached to their watches and the butcher threw in a slice of liver for the cat when he wrapped up the meat order, then you are close to establishing the date of the Golden Age of Secret Remedies. No family circle was complete without the brown or green bottle on sideboard or shelf. Sometimes the contents were murky, mysterious, evil in taste and smell. Sometimes they looked like whiskey, smelled like whiskey, and tasted like whiskey, for the best of reasons: they *were* whiskey. The presence of generous amounts of ethyl alcohol was necessary, according to a familiar explanation, for the "preservation" of the medicinal ingredients. Two

*OPPOSITE: Versatile John C. Hurst treated everything from tuberculosis to scuffed shoes. Merchants Gargling Oil, above, was also a liniment for men, mules, and horses; hence the horseshoe.*

tablespoonfuls, taken before a meal, produced an agreeable sense of well-being or levitation, that walking-on-air feeling often associated with a dollop of the Good Creature.

This was the period—call it the early 1900's—when beards signified age and wisdom, the learned professions. So the home panaceas usually portrayed on their labels the luxurious whiskers of the doctor-proprietor. His license was of obscure origin. But there wasn't anything obscure about his ownership of the name of his cure-all or his indignant fulminations against designing men who plotted to steal his customers with a similar article. Their claims were fraudulent because *his* medicine was patented.

The idea of proprietary medicines being patented is a stubborn bit of American folklore, accepted for generations as gospel truth and even repeated recently as a serious definition by the distinguished *American Heritage Dictionary of the English Language* in these words: "*patent*

By GERALD CARSON

19

*medicine.* A drug or other medical preparation that is protected by a patent and can be bought without a prescription."

A few patent applications were made, it is true, in the very early days of the United States Patent Office, when the law was first drawn and the examiners were not discriminating. Between 1793 and 1836, especially, papers were filed by rustic applicants who did not understand their grave error in revealing, as they were required to do, the ingredients they used. Disclosure of the formula was the last thing an experienced promoter had in mind, since his concoction would be immediately recognized either as harmful or as an innocuous granny remedy like sarsaparilla syrup mixed with oil of wintergreen flavoring. If a patent was applied for and granted, a new difficulty then arose. The formula would by law become public property in seventeen years—a sure way of going out of business and losing all the good will built up by years of gaudy advertising.

What the owners of nostrums (literal meaning: "our own") were really interested in was not the contents of the bottle, which were subject to change without notice and were of very minor consequence, but the legal protection of the trademark. This was achieved by patenting the unique shape of the bottle and by copyrighting the design of the label and the printed matter wrapped around the package. Before the copyright law existed, the trade name could be defended under common law. After it became registerable (but not patentable) in the Patent Office, the name became a property whose ownership didn't lapse after a mere seventeen years but could be monopolized for all eternity.

The contents of the bottle changed with changing circumstances. For example, when the United States Treasury ruled that Peruna, a little gold mine owned by genial Dr. Samuel B. Hartman, of Columbus, Ohio, must have a detectable medicinal effect or face taxation as a straight alcoholic beverage, the doctor, a former Bible salesman, complied by dumping generous amounts of blackthorn bark, a powerful cathartic, into the Peruna retorts. There followed a national rumbling of the bowels that was heard from Maine to California, but especially in those

*A decorous Pinkham advertising card.* OPPOSITE PAGE: *Lydia herself as she appeared in an early cabinet photograph.*

states where citizens preferred taking their *spiritus frumenti* under an alias. They could feel secure in the knowledge, gained from advertisements in their church papers, that the nostrum was recommended by "An Indefatigable and Life-long Worker in the Temperance Cause."

When our century was young, nearly every drug, notions, or general merchandise store had a special patent-medicine department, arranged alongside the horse and poultry remedies. This was not incongruous because many of the medicines were, like Dr. Bennett's Golden Liniment, "for horses . . . equally as efficacious as upon the human family." One honest druggist, George "Pop" Stansfield, of Topeka, Kansas, received national attention when he displayed a large sign in his store that announced: "We sell patent medicines but do not recommend them." Another skeptic, also from Kansas, was E. W. Howe, the sage of Atchison, who took notice of Dr. David Jayne, the Philadelphia tapeworm king, in a characteristic paragraph in his Atchison *Globe:* "Every time we see big, fat George Shifflett, we can't help laughing over the fact that when he isn't feeling well, his wife makes him take Jayne's Vermifuge, a worm medicine for children."

But Dr. Jayne could laugh, too. His dark-brown-tasting mixture in the green oval bottle built a $300,000 mansion with doors of solid walnut and silver door-knobs and with his daughters' faces sculptured on every mantel. When he died, it took a will of twenty-five pages to disburse his three million dollars' worth of assets.

Many fortuitous circumstances came together in the mid-nineteenth century to make it possible for a young shoemaker or bookbinder with a formula for a lung balsam or corn cure, an intuitive grasp of popular psychology, and an elastic conscience to make a fortune and leave behind a catchy-sounding trade name like Radway's Ready Relief or Hostetter's Celebrated Stomach Bitters, often good for a run of a hundred years. There was, first of all, a splendid propaganda opening provided by the airing of tedious quarrels between rival schools of regular medicine. Other factors favorable to the "patents" were the rapid spread of literacy, cheap postage, improvements in printing and graphic reproduction, the extension of the national railroad network, and, oddly enough, the development of the religious press. And war. The wounds and diseases of the veterans who survived the Civil War introduced into the community-at-large new mental patterns of fear and faith—fear of ill health and regular doctors, a touching faith in Dr. Williams' Pink Pills for Pale People. Or Hostetter's Bitters. The War Department bought this stomachic in carload lots for the Union armies. It remained a medical standby of the Grand Army of the Republic for decades and supported four generations of Hostetters in a state of affluence to which they easily accustomed themselves.

By the 1880's self-made doctors, wandering Indians, and cleverly personalized corporations were catering to every imaginable pathology or fantasy with lost-manhood tablets, bust developers, dyspepsia pills, abortifacients, and tuberculosis "cures." They also produced treatments for a class of diseases delicately associated with "youthful indiscretions." All employed the same propagandistic devices: spreading skepticism of the medical profession, overwhelming the patient with sympathy, parading the testimonials of those who honestly believed they had been benefited, while subtly inducing by suggestion the frightening symptoms so graphically described on the label. The literature of the proprietaries threatened, scolded, and confused those who were sick or worried, but catered always to their determination to make their own diagnosis of what ailed them.

A major theme was a condition known as female weakness. Under this vague phrase were gathered all the ills of the female physiology and psyche. The most gifted healer who worked this vein was Mrs. Lydia E. Pinkham, who found her fortune and apotheosis in a herb medicine of her own concoction, Lydia E. Pinkham's Vegetable Compound. "Only a woman," declared Lydia, "can understand a woman's ills," a characteristically pithy observation loaded with overtones of feminine rebellion and hostility to men.

Mrs. Pinkham, whom publicist Elbert Hubbard compared favorably with Florence Nightingale, Clara Barton, Julia Ward Howe, Harriet Beecher Stowe, Dorothea Dix, Joan of Arc, and other notables, is well worth meeting. Lydia Pinkham, née Estes, the daughter of a shoe-maker, was born February 9, 1819, in Lynn, Massachusetts. In this "City of Shoes" there also flourished other remarkable women, such as Susan B. Anthony, Mary Baker Eddy, and Mrs. Mary Sergeant Neal Gove, the water-cure physician and reformer, who introduced to Lynn the bloomer costume and brown-bread supper, hard beds, mesmerism, and free love. Educated locally, Lydia bubbled with the heady doctrines that were floating in the air of eastern Massachusetts like wild yeasts—Swedenborgianism, phrenology, temperance, Sylvester Graham's vegetarian faith, women's rights, spirtualism, botanic medicine, and fiat money.

Married in 1843 to an ineffectual husband, Isaac Pinkham, Mrs. Pinkham had four sons, three of whom she survived, and a daughter. When Mr. Pinkham's chief occupation proved to be losing money in real estate, Lydia, in desperation, put her hand to supporting the family. Like many New England housewives Mrs. Pinkham had prepared her own home remedies—fennel teas, rhubarb cathartics, and the like. But the winner was her "vegetable" nostrum for the indispositions of the female reproductive apparatus. For years she had boiled and strained her sovereign remedy in the home kitchen and given it away as a gesture of neighborliness. But after the 1873 panic, with her family in actual want, Lydia turned professional. The Vegetable Compound made its commercial debut in 1875. Early in 1876 a label was registered in the Patent Office. Later the government found that the "sure cure" contained 17.9 per cent alcohol and 0.56 grains of vegetable extractive material to each 100 c.c., consisting of such squaw-medicine therapeutic agents as Alestris (True Unicorn) and Asclepias (Pleurisy Root), which had disappeared from the United States *Pharmacopoeia* some forty years before. But even the harshest critics of the Vegetable Compound never claimed that it did its users any harm, though they insisted that it didn't do any good, either.

The Pinkham children filled and corked the bottles and folded handbills. Mother got up the medicine and demonstrated a real flair for publicity. Son Dan, too, was touched with promotional genius. One of his ideas was to scatter little cards in the parks of Brooklyn, New York, "so small . . ." he pointed out in a family letter, "that it

21

# "OH-H-H, we'll sing of Lydia Pinkham..."

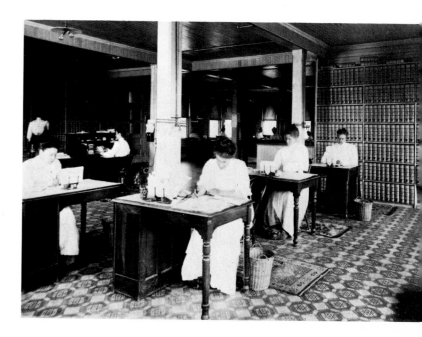

*Lydia E. Pinkham* ®

# LYDIA E.
# PINKHAM
## VEGETABLE
# COMPOUND

For relieving hot flashes and certain other symptoms associated with "Change of Life" (Menopause) and cramps and other distress of Monthly Periods (Menstruation) — not due to organic disease. Acts as a uterine sedative.

Piscidia Erythrina (Jamaica Dogwood), Asclepias Tuberosa (Pleurisy Root), Cimicifuga Racemosa (Black Cohosh), Senecio Aureus (Life Root), Glycyrrhiza (Licorice), Taraxacum Officinale (Dandelion), Gentiana Lutea (Gentian), Thiamin Hydrochloride (Vitamin $B_1$), 13½% Ethyl Alcohol (used solely as a solvent and preservative).

Taken as directed, supplies 333 U.S.P. units (1 mg.) Thiamin Hydrochloride (Vitamin $B_1$) per day (minimum adult daily requirement).

LYDIA E. PINKHAM MEDICINE COMPANY
LYNN, MASSACHUSETTS, U. S. A.

CONTENTS 7 FL. OZ.
207 C.C.

*The claims to cure tumors and what-have-you seen on the early package on the left, page 22, are typical of the uninhibited advertising that prevailed before the passage of the Pure Food and Drug Act. The first Pinkham factory and the family home appear in that order at top right, same page. The sign hanging from the Brooklyn Bridge, center, existed, of course, only in the imagination of the Pinkhams. The woman-to-woman tone of Lydia's advertisements led to a vast correspondence, carried on by an all-girl staff, seen at bottom left. Mrs. Pinkham died in 1883, but her genes flourished again in the person of son Charles, seen above standing at left by the wagon. Grandson Arthur sits on the horse. The factory, built in 1886, is still turning out the compound. Today's package, right, disclaims having any effect upon organic disease. The alcoholic content is 13½ per cent, slightly more than that of a table wine. If the famous nostrum is no longer a sure cure for all the afflictions of the "female system," it is still a reasonably potent drink regardless of the gender of the imbiber.*

wouldn't pay for rag and paper pickers to pick them up"; another gambit, which worked out very well, was to drop personal notes, appearing to have been accidentally lost, in cemeteries just before the Memorial Day crowds arrived. The notes urgently recommended, of course, the regular use of Lydia's "Greatest Remedy in the World." But the gut idea was to put Mrs. Pinkham's picture on the package, right above where it said "Contains 18 per cent of Alcohol." How Lydia, an enthusiastic member of the w.c.t.u., adjusted her principles to this generous infusion of spirits, or how, being a Victorian lady, she endured the exploitation of her picture, history does not disclose. No doubt she found that the end justified the means. At any rate, she died rich in worldly goods, which became the subject of bitter litigation among the surviving Pinkham stockholders. Lydia was blessed also in the gifts of the spirit, for she was friend, confidante, and benefactress of untold thousands of women who had some maladjustment in their lives and had responded gratefully to her invitation to "Write to Mrs. Pinkham."

In the last quarter of the nineteenth century, when country editors were not well supplied with portraits of prominent women, the electrotype of Mrs. Pinkham was often the only one to be found in the print shop, with the result that her face was presented at one time or another as a recent picture of Lily Langtry, as Dr. Mary Walker, the lady who wore men's trousers, as President Cleveland's new bride, as Sarah Bernhardt, and even as Queen Victoria. The cast-iron smile of the famous picture, the black silk dress with a bit of white ruching at the neck, the evident sincerity and respectability of homey, trustworthy, sadly sweet Mrs. Pinkham, tickled the national sense of humor. There were Pinkham jokes and editorial pleasantries. Bill Nye, the professional humorist, nominated Mrs. Pinkham for President; college boys wrote in pseudonymously for advice on timidity, frigidity, and similar intimate matters, and they sang merrily in fraternity houses, to the tune of the old Gospel hymn, "I Will Sing of My Redeemer":

> *Tell me, Lydia, of your secrets,*
> *And the wonders you perform,*
> *How you take the sick and ailing*
> *And restore them to the norm?*

TEXT CONTINUES ON PAGE 108
ILLUSTRATIONS CONTINUE OVERLEAF

*A great "card craze" swept the United States between the 1870's and the 90's. These cardboard lithographs pictured blooming children and domestic scenes that associated the illustration with the product. "Paste them in your album," Mrs. Pinkham advised in distributing the trade card of two of her grandchildren seen at the top of this page. The text printed on the verso of the cards got down to the main business: sickness, symptoms, and cure.*

24

# Women and Children First

HE WANTS IT.

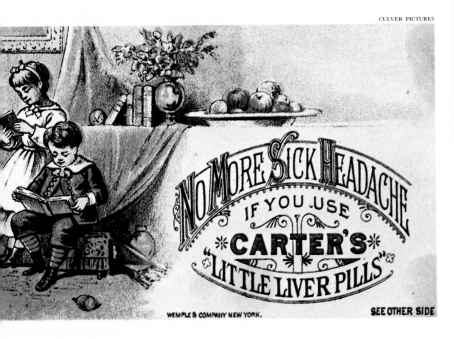

CULVER PICTURES

HELMBOLD'S FLUID EXTRACT OF BUCHU.

HOTTENTOTS

HOTTENTOTS

Seen gathering Buchu Leaves at the Cape of Good Hope for

**H. T. HELMBOLD, Druggist,**
**594 Broadway, New York.**

At the Cape of Good Hope the Hottentots have long used Buchu for a variety of diseases; it was borrowed from those rude practitioners by the English and Dutch physicians, on whose recommendation it was employed in Europe, and has now come into general use. It is given chiefly in gravel, chronic catarrh of the bladder, morbid irritation of the bladder and urethra, for female weakness and debility, for prolapsus and bearing down, or prolapsus uteri, diseases of the prostate gland, retention or incontinence of urine, and all diseases requiring the aid of a diuretic arising from a loss of tone in the parts concerned in its evacuation. It is also recommended in cases of dyspepsia, chronic rheumatism, cutaneous affections, and dropsy. To cure these diseases we must bring into action the muscles which are engaged in their various functions. To neglect them, however slight may be the attack, it is sure to affect the bodily health and mental powers. Our *flesh and blood are supported from these sources.* Persons at every period of life, *from infancy to old age,* and in every state of health, are liable to be subjects of these diseases. The causes in many instances are unknown. The patient has, however, an admirable remedy in "Helmbold's Fluid Extract of Buchu," and when taken in early stages of the disease none suffer to any extent. It allays pain and inflammation, is free from all injurious properties, pleasant in its taste and odor, and immediate in its action. It is the anchor of hope to the physician, and was always so esteemed by the late eminent Dr. Physic. The proprietor, with upwards of thirty thousand unsolicited certificates, and hundreds of thousands of living witnesses of its curative properties, accumulated within fifteen years, has not been in the habit of resorting to their publication. He does not do this from the fact that his remedies rank as standard; they do not need to be *propped up by certificates. The science of medicine, like the Doric column, should stand simple, pure, and majestic, having fact for its basis, induction for its pillar, and truth alone for its capital.* His Solid and Fluid Extracts embody the full strength of the ingredients of which they are named. They are left to the inspection of all. A ready and conclusive test of their properties will be a comparison with those set forth in the United States Dispensatory. These remedies are prepared by H. T. Helmbold, Druggist of sixteen years' experience, and we believe them to be reliable—in fact, we have never known an article lacking merit to meet with a permanent success, and Mr. Helmbold's success is certainly prima facia evidence. His Drug and Chemical Warehouse in the city of New York is not excelled, if equaled, by any in this country, and we would advise our readers when visiting that city to give him a call and judge for themselves.—*N. Y. Times, October 2, 1861.*

The African plant buchu and the Hottentots, left, made flamboyant Henry T. Helmbold rich and famous and enabled him to mingle with such celebrities as Boss Tweed, the Shah of Persia, and President U. S. Grant. The greatest push behind the remedies of London-born Thomas Holloway, one of whose broadsides is shown below right, was the Civil War with its wounds, injuries, and diseases. The Indian medicine show, lower left, provided free entertainment plus the clinical pitch until well into this century, a picturesque fragment of the American past. Political endorsement, right, was frequently sought by the titans of proprietary medicine, and easily obtained.

BROWN BROTHERS

LIBRARY OF CONGRESS

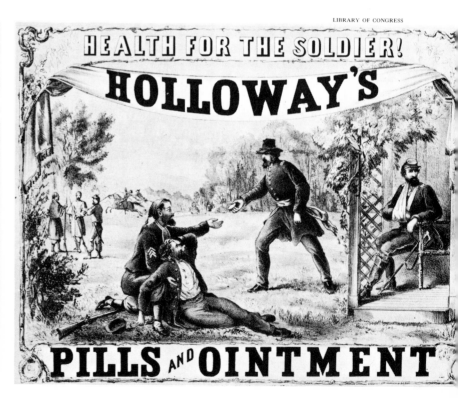

HEALTH FOR THE SOLDIER!
HOLLOWAY'S
PILLS AND OINTMENT

INAUGURATION OF GOV. GEORGE D. ROBINSON.

Gov. Robinson says:–! Benjamin, at the beginning of the Campaign I was all broken down, and a beaten man, but "Sulphur Bitters" gave me enough strength to beat you.
Ex Gov. Butler says:–! Yes! Yes! George, if I had only taken "Sulphur Bitters" this year as I did last, I should have beaten you as bad as I did Bishop.

# Echoes of the Little Bighorn

*The author in 1948, flanked by Little Bighorn alumni: left to right, Little Warrior, Pemmican, Little Soldier, Dewey Beard, John Sitting Bull, Joseph High Eagle, Iron Hawk, Comes Again.*

PORTRAITS AND TEXT ·

*by* DAVID HUMPHREYS MILLER

*No single battle in American history has won more attention from more writers than the relatively insignificant defeat of a handful of cavalry by a few thousand Indians on the Little Bighorn River in 1876. How could there be anything new to say about it? Yet there is—the recollections of the Indians themselves—and that is the story we have to tell in this collection of reminiscences gathered before the survivors all died and translated by David Humphreys Miller, the author of several books on Indians, including* Custer's Fall *(Duell, Sloan & Pearce, 1957), and a writer for motion pictures. An artist as well, Mr. Miller has done all that any man can to bring to life once again this desperate moment in American history.*

Indian country—the sprawling Sioux and Cheyenne reservations—lured me to the Dakotas and Montana in 1935, when I was sixteen. Having sketched, painted, and written since I was old enough to hold pencil or brush, I was prepared to fill many sketchbooks and notebooks with all I expected to see and hear.

The historic Battle of the Little Bighorn had occurred fifty-nine years earlier, so I calculated there still must be Indian survivors of Custer's Last Stand who could tell me their side of the story. My high school history books dealt sparingly, if at all, with the Indian wars of the Plains. It seemed vital in exploring the past to find old-timers who had actually lived the battle.

I soon discovered that none of the older Indians I wished to depict and interview spoke English, and it soon became obvious that the language barrier and constant need for an interpreter would be a handicap in securing full and complete statements. Already armed with a knowledge of the indispensable sign language every old Plains Indian used, I assiduously studied the Sioux tongue and, later, Cheyenne, Arapaho, Crow, Blackfoot, and Kiowa, as I came into contact with those tribes.

Overcoming the linguistic hurdle opened the minds and memories of the old warriors to me as nothing else could and, moreover, helped ameliorate their still considerable resentment and distrust of white men generally. Tribes that had fought the frontier army and had finally been defeated were shabbily treated; even in the thirties many of these former "hostiles" were starving. I did what I could to help them, shared their privations, and gradually won their confidence. I was formally adopted into five Plains tribes and made a "relative" by many Indian families.

Some old-timers, however, still clung to the superstition that if their likenesses were sketched, painted, or photographed, part of their souls would leave them to go with their portraits. One bitter old Sioux named Crazy Bull refused for more than a year to submit to an interview or sit for his portrait. Appealing to his somewhat rusty sense of humor, I finally won his cautious friendship and trust, although I deliberately refrained from asking him again to pose or to engage in anything but small talk. Then one day he came to ask *me* to paint his likeness and listen to his story of Little Bighorn.

In all, I interviewed seventy-one old-timers in their seventies, eighties, and nineties who had taken part in the Custer fight: fifty-four Sioux, sixteen Cheyennes, and one Arapaho. I questioned them in their own languages and found, with very few exceptions, that none of them had ever before told their stories to a white man or had their portraits painted. It was my purpose to tax their memories. Whenever possible, I arranged joint conferences with several survivors, who often reminded each other of various details that might otherwise have been overlooked. It was considered bad form, however, for any warrior to talk of something he had not personally seen or done. At the same time their somewhat complicated system of tabulating battle honors and counting coups required reliable witnesses, and sometimes two or three interviews were necessary to crosscheck certain points against the white soldiers' version in the military annals. However, since Little Bighorn was the greatest battle of these warlike Indians, I was not surprised to find their recollections of it honest and lucid. After all, no white man survived to tell of Custer's final hour; only these Indians who fought him could describe the climactic events.

The matter of which Indian killed Custer has bothered generations of historians. It may simply boil down to a question of identity. White Bull was firmly convinced, I am sure, that he had killed Long Hair, for he had undoubtedly slain a leader of the soldiers who wore a buckskin jacket after this white man had fired twice at him and missed. But White Bull may have been unaware that Custer's brothers, Tom and Boston, who died with him, also wore buckskin jackets, or that officers Yates, Cooke, Smith, Porter, Calhoun, and possibly Keogh wore buckskin blouses (as described in a special report dated January 16, 1896, by General—then Major—E. S. Godfrey). The leader White Bull killed could have been any of these men, for no warrior knew Long Hair was on the field until *after* the fight. Only a handful of hostiles had ever seen Custer, who at his wife's request had had his flowing locks, his frontier trademark and most identifying feature, trimmed short before the battle.

Dewey Beard may also have been honestly mistaken in his identification of Long Hair, although I do not question his testimony that he *thought* the white man killed by Charging Hawk was the leader of the soldiers.

White Cow Bull did not claim to have killed Long Hair, but to have shot a man, whom he later heard called Long Hair, out of his saddle at the ford. While never mentioned in kill-talks after the battle as Custer's slayer, he may well have been the warrior who inflicted Custer's mortal wound. His story satisfies several enigmas, accounting for the troopers' halt in midcharge and their abrupt shift from offensive attack to defensive and apparently demoralized retreat. Two hundred fifteen hell-for-leather cavalrymen would scarcely have turned back *unless* they had suddenly found themselves with a dead or mortally wounded leader. The loss of any other officer would hardly have had such a deleterious effect.

The fact that Custer's body, according to both Indian and white accounts, was later found on the west slope of the ridge to which his troops retreated fails to prove that he was killed or mortally wounded on the spot. Accepting the validity of White Cow Bull's statement that Long Hair fell at the ford actually provides an explanation for the body's location. Only Custer's body would have been carried by the troops as they fell back.

In early kill-talks after the battle several other warriors claimed to have slain Long Hair: Red Horse, a Miniconjou; Flat Hip, a Hunkpapa; and Walks-Under-the-Ground, a Santee—probably because he wound up in possession of Custer's horse. Little Knife, a Hunkpapa, said Brown Back killed Custer to avenge his brother Deeds, who had been killed by soldiers early the day of the fight. Two sons of *Inkpaduta* (Scarlet Tip), chief of the Santee, made a joint claim. Fast Eagle, an Oglala, said he held Custer's arms while Walking Blanket Woman, the girl warrior, stabbed Long Hair in the back. Charging Hawk, a Miniconjou, did not deny the deed when others (including Dewey Beard) declared they saw him kill the soldier chief. Three Northern Cheyennes—Two Moon, Harshay Wolf, and Medicine Bear—claimed they counted coup on Custer but admitted they did not see him die.

Whites were properly confused by this plethora of claims. Such an enterprising showman as Buffalo Bill Cody attempted to credit Sitting Bull—who turned out to be so affable a showman himself that few believed in his villainy.

Eventually as perplexed as white entrepreneurs, poets, and historians, Indian leaders of eleven tribes settled the matter in characteristic fashion—and to their satisfaction—in September, 1909, when the wealthy Philadelphian Rodman Wanamaker gathered them in conclave for a last Great Council on the Little Bighorn. He offered a considerable largesse to be prorated among them if one of those present could prove himself to be Custer's killer. After days of deliberation in secret council, mulling over conflicting claims, the chiefs found the record of a sixty-four-year-old Southern Cheyenne war chief made to order: not only had Chief Brave Bear fought at Little Bighorn; he had earlier fought Custer at the Battle of the Washita in 1868, a defeat for his people that provided him with a fitting motive for evening the score. After lengthy palaver the council unanimously *elected* Brave Bear the honorary slayer of Long Hair Custer!

The Battle of the Little Bighorn, on June 25, 1876, has had its impact on history for ninety-five years. Its endless ramifications may well continue to fascinate historians and laymen alike for more generations to come. Undoubtedly, the Custer fight will long remain the apotheosis of the adventurous American spirit. —*D.H.M.*

## HENRY OSCAR ONE BULL

Chief Henry Oscar One Bull was the first Indian veteran of the Battle of the Little Bighorn to pose for me and tell me his version of the Custer fight. I located him at an Indian pageant south of Rapid City, South Dakota, in the mid-1930's. As a nephew, adopted son, and body-guard of the great Sioux chief Sitting Bull, he had held an elevated position in the hierarchy of Indian command.

Well past eighty at our first meeting,* One Bull was withered and bent with age, his legs widely bowed from long years on horseback. He was still remarkably agile in the saddle, but he walked only with the aid of a pol-ished cottonwood cane. On ceremonial occasions the cane also served as a scepter of his authority as the last hereditary chief of the Hunkpapa tribe—the northern-most and traditionally the most warlike of the entire Sioux nation. As a badge of his distinction as a warrior he tied to the cane a buffalo-hide shield, painted white and decorated with blue lightning streaks. Eagle feathers fluttered from the shield's rim.

In the summer of 1938 I made my annual visit to the Crow Indian Fair at Crow Agency, Montana—an event that in prewar years attracted thousands of Indians from all over the country. To my delight I found that One Bull and his family were among them. Since the Custer Battlefield was a short drive from our camp, I was deter-mined to take advantage of the Chief's presence and in-vited him to show me over the fighting ground, step by step. He gladly complied, pointing out where each of the

*He died at ninety-four, in 1947.

great camp circles had been, where the soldiers had come charging in initial phases of the battle, and where he had won individual honors as a warrior. We even looked in vain for a cache of captured bullets One Bull said he had buried under some rocks along the river. Back in camp he told me his story, conversing, as usual, in Sioux:

It was the time when ponies are fat [June]. During a sun dance we held on Rosebud Creek ten days earlier, my uncle, Sitting Bull, had offered a hundred pieces of his flesh to *Wakantanka* [Great Holy Spirit] and had been granted a vision of white soldiers without ears falling upside-down into camp. He told me that this vision was a promise of a great victory yet to come. Three days later we beat Gray Fox [General George Crook] in a fight on the Rosebud. But my uncle said an even greater vic-tory was coming.

The night before the fight with Long Hair, Sitting Bull went out to the ridge where the monument now stands. He sang a thunder song, then prayed for knowledge of things to come. As he repeated for me later, he wailed aloud, offering a filled pipe as he prayed:

"*Wakantanka*, hear me and pity me! I offer you this pipe in the name of my people. Save them. We want to live! Guard my people against all danger and misfortune. Take pity on us!"

Then he stuck slender wands in the ground to which he tied tiny buckskin bags of tobacco and willow bark. Next day Long Hair's horse soldiers would knock them all down, but that night my uncle knew that *Wakantanka* had heard his prayer. Before sunup an old woman died in the Hunkpapa camp. She was the wife of Sitting Bull's uncle, Four Horns. As Sitting Bull later told me, the death of such an important woman made him wonder if the promised victory might not come that very day.

I was twenty-three that summer and had been a warrior a long time. Another Hunkpapa named Gray Eagle and I were Sitting Bull's special bodyguards. It was our duty to watch him and see that he had protection. I also had the duty of seeing that his orders were carried out by others and to look after his property. That morning I took the family horses to the river.

At midday I went back to the pony herd and drove the horses to the river for the noon watering. Just then I heard shooting near the Hunkpapa camp circle. I knew our camp soldiers [police] did not allow offhand firing. So I recognized the shots as a warning of some kind of danger. I quickly caught my best pony and turned the other stock loose, knowing they would head back to camp as soon as the hobbles were off. Not far away I saw dust rising and heard iron-shod hoofs pounding against loose rocks. I raced back to the tepee I shared with my uncle.

The Hunkpapa camp was in an uproar. Warriors were rush-ing around to catch their ponies. Women were screaming and children were crying and old men were shouting advice as loud as they could. Then the women and children began to run off to the west, not taking the time to strike their tepees or to carry off belongings.

I reached the tepee ahead of my uncle. I grabbed my old muzzleloader and quickly checked it. Just then Sitting Bull entered the tepee and took the old rifle out of my hands. He handed me a stone-headed war club, then took his own rawhide shield out of its buckskin case and hung it over my shoulder. This shield was both for protection and to be used as a badge of the chief's authority.

"You will take my place and go out and meet the soldiers that are attacking us," he ordered. "Parley with them, if you can. If they are willing, tell them I will talk peace with them."

Sitting Bull was buckling on his cartridge belt as we hurried outside. His deaf-mute adopted son came running up with the chief's black stallion. Another bodyguard, named Iron Elk, handed my uncle a Winchester carbine and a revolver and held the stallion's jaw rope. Sitting Bull jumped on the stallion's bare back and galloped off to look for his old mother and get her to safety. Many young warriors gathered around me. I raised my uncle's shield high so they all could see it. Then I led them out to meet the soldiers.

One Bull soon discovered that any talk of peace with Major Marcus A. Reno's attacking troopers was out of the question. Soldiers now on the firing line began shooting as soon as they saw the raised shield. Ree [Arikara] Indian scouts, serving the 7th Cavalry, were trying to capture the huge herd of Sioux ponies west of the camp. Chief Black Moon rode up with a large force of Hunkpapa camp police to save the pony herd. One Bull rallied his warriors for a charge.

The Sioux onslaught began suddenly, sweeping back the Ree scouts and halting Reno's advance. Black Moon's Hunkpapas hit Reno's exposed flank. As One Bull told me:

The soldiers were mixed up. Some got off their horses and began firing again as we rode in. Others stayed mounted. Two soldiers couldn't hold their horses in all the excitement. The horses bolted, carrying their riders right into our warriors. These soldiers didn't last long!

Then the soldier chief shouted something, and all the soldiers did a strange thing. They all got off their horses, except for every fourth man who held the horses for the other three. Then they ran on foot trying to get into the timber along the river. I raised my uncle's shield again and led another charge to chase them. They were turning around to shoot at us, but we rode right into them, chasing them into the river. We killed many on the river bank and in the water.

I rode up behind one soldier and knocked him over with my war club. Then I slid off my pony and held the soldier's head under water until he was dead. I killed two more soldiers in the water.

A Hunkpapa warrior named Good Bear Boy was riding alongside me and was suddenly shot off his horse. Black Moon fell about the same time. He was dead, but Good Bear Boy was only wounded. I ordered a warrior named Looking Elk to rescue him, but Looking Elk didn't hear me. Good Bear Boy tried to crawl back from the river.

I saw many soldiers struggle across the river and climb out on the far bank. They ran to a high butte [now called Reno Hill], and from there they kept shooting at us. Some of them dug holes [trenches] in the ground and got into these holes or behind their saddles so we couldn't hit them. I ordered warriors

to surround the butte so the soldiers couldn't get away. I wanted to starve them out. A Lakota told me later that the warriors kept those soldiers there all night. Finally, the soldiers began to get crazy for water. The Lakotas [Teton Sioux] wouldn't let the soldiers go to the river to drink or get water to take back up to their holes in the ground. Two or three of them tried to crawl down to the river, but our warriors shot them.

Bullets were flying all around, but I saw that Good Bear Boy wasn't able to crawl back to camp. He was shot through both thighs and bleeding heavily. So I jumped off my pony long enough to help Good Bear Boy climb on, then I leaped up behind him. I heard my pony scream. A bullet had struck his hindquarters. I took Good Bear Boy back to camp and saw that his friends took care of him. As I left him, I saw three soldiers running on foot toward the river. They had gotten away from us earlier in the fight. I charged after them, and they ran very fast. I wanted to ride them down, but just then I heard my uncle's voice.

"O, come back, my son!" he shouted.

Sitting Bull had seen the blood of Good Bear Boy and my pony all over my legs and thought I was wounded. Then he said: "Let them go! Let them live to tell the truth about this fight!"

I obeyed. We let the three soldiers escape. My uncle looked worried.

"Nephew, you are wounded. Go to the women and have your wounds treated."

So I laughed, saying I wasn't wounded and telling him about Good Bear Boy.

"You have done well. You put up a good fight. Now go help defend the women and children and old ones. More soldiers may come."

I did as he ordered and joined our people west of the camp. Soon after I reached them, I saw more dust across the river. A second band of soldiers was riding down a coulee toward the ford by the Miniconjou camp circle. Another alarm went up. I saw a handful of warriors racing to the ford to meet them. Then more warriors left the soldiers surrounded on the butte and galloped over to head off this second attack. They chased these new soldiers out of the coulee and up onto a long ridge. More of our warriors, mostly Oglalas and Cheyennes, were waiting for these soldiers at the end of the ridge and caught them in a trap. They were all wiped out in a short time. My brother White Bull later said the leader of this second band of soldiers was Long Hair Custer. White Bull was fighting the soldiers on the ridge and he can tell you about that part of the battle.

Reno's troops, reinforced by Captain Frederick W. Benteen's detachment and a pack train of ammunition, were kept surrounded on the butte throughout that night and until noon the following day. Had the Indians attacked them in force, from all directions, there is little doubt that the remainder of the 7th Cavalry would have been wiped out to a man. As One Bull told me, however, Sitting Bull ordered the warriors to stop fighting:

*Henala!* Enough!" my uncle shouted. "Those soldiers are trying to live, so let them live. Let them go. If we kill all of them, a bigger army will march against us."

## JOSEPH WHITE COW BULL

The old man sat cross-legged in the Montana sun, posing for me with his gaunt shoulders draped in an ancient trade-cloth blanket, gnarled fingers clutching a cottonwood cane. It was hard to imagine that his scraggy hands had once been dexterous with firearms, or that his watery eyes, with bluish, washed-out irises, had been among the keenest of any warrior's who had fought in the Battle of the Little Bighorn.

We were camped that August day in 1938 at the Crow Fair. His name was Joseph White Cow Bull. An Oglala Sioux from Pine Ridge Indian Reservation in South Dakota, he had come to have a last look at the battlefield before he died.

His name seemed somewhat anomalous in combining the bovine sexes. It made better sense in Sioux than it did in English. *Ptebloka Ska* indicated a male of the white man's semidomesticated longhorn cattle, which some interpreter, lacking fluency in English, had evidently mistranslated. White Cow Bull, I learned, had earned the name at age fourteen by shooting a stray longhorn bull with a single arrow.

My first portrait sketch of him completed, I loaded the old man in my car and headed south out of camp on U.S. Highway 87, by-passing the entrance to Custer Battlefield and National Cemetery so he could first see the site of the great Indian village where he had camped sixty-two years earlier. I realized that time and cultivation by the semiagricultural Crow must have caused considerable changes in the look of the land. White Cow Bull nonetheless soon managed to point out where the wide camp circles, each a half mile in diameter, had sprawled along the Little Bighorn River.

Spreading his hands to indicate a large circle, he said:

The *Shahiyela* [Cheyenne] camp was farthest north. We Oglala were camped just southeast of them, with the Brulé in a smaller circle next to us. Next were the Sans Arc, then the Miniconjou, the Blackfoot Sioux, and farthest south next to the river were the Hunkpapa. I was twenty-eight years old that summer.

While we were together in this village, I spent most of my time with the *Shahiyela* since I knew their tongue and their ways almost as well as my own. In all those years I had never taken a wife, although I had had many women. One woman I wanted was a pretty young *Shahiyela* named Monahseetah, or Meotzi as I called her. She was in her middle twenties but had never married any man of her tribe. Some of my *Shahiyela* friends said she was from the southern branch of their tribe, just visiting up north, and they said no *Shahiyela* could marry her because she had a seven-year-old son born out of wedlock and that tribal law forbade her getting married. They said the boy's father had been a white soldier chief named Long Hair; he had killed her father, Chief Black Kettle, in a battle in the south [Battle of the Washita] eight winters before, they said, and captured her. He had told her he wanted to make her his second wife, and so he had her. But after while his first wife, a white woman, found her out and made him let her go.

"Was this boy still with her here?" I asked him.

Yes, I saw him often around the *Shahiyela* camp. He was named Yellow Bird and he had light streaks in his hair. He was always with his mother in the daytime, so I would have to wait until night to try to talk to her alone. She knew I wanted to walk with her under a courting blanket and make her my wife. But she would only talk with me through the tepee cover and never came outside.

White Cow Bull sat silent a few minutes, musing on the past, I suppose, and remembering the Cheyenne girl Long Hair Custer had dishonored in the eyes of her people. Later interviews corroborated the old Oglala's statement that Monahseetah and Yellow Bird had been in the Little Bighorn camp at the time of the fight, many of my Cheyenne informants insisting that their strict moral code, more rigid than that of the Sioux, imposed restrictions on their relationships with fallen women. I was already familiar with various accounts of Custer's winter campaign against the Southern Cheyenne in 1868, in several of which Monahseetah is mentioned as having served Custer as an interpreter—although she apparently then spoke no English!

"Tell me about the battle with Long Hair," I said.

That morning many of the Oglalas were sleeping late. The night before, we held a scalp dance to celebrate the victory over Gray Fox [General Crook] on the Rosebud a week before. I woke up hungry and went to a nearby tepee to ask an old woman for food. As I ate, she said:

"Today attackers are coming."

"How do you know, Grandmother?" I asked her, but she would say nothing more about it.

After I finished eating I caught my best pony, an iron-gray gelding, and rode over to the Cheyenne camp circle. I looked all over for Meotzi and finally saw her carrying firewood up from the river. The boy was with her, so I just smiled and said nothing. I rode on to visit with my *Shahiyela* friend Roan Bear. He was a Fox warrior, belonging to one of that tribe's soldier societies, and was on guard duty that morning. He was stationed by the *Shahiyela* medicine tepee in which the tribe kept their Sacred Buffalo Head. . . . We settled down to telling each other some of our brave deeds in the past. The morning went by quickly, for an Elk warrior named Bobtail Horse joined us to tell us stories about his chief, Dull Knife, who was not there that day.

The first we knew of any attack was after midday, when we saw dust and heard shooting way to the south near the Hunkpapa camp circle. . . .

Just then an Oglala came riding into the circle at a gallop.

"Soldiers are coming!" he shouted in Sioux. "Many white men are attacking!"

I put this into a shout of *Shahiyela* words so they would know. I saw the *Shahiyela* chief, Two Moon, run into camp from the river, leading three or four horses. He hurried toward his tepee, yelling:

"*Nutskaveho!* White soldiers are coming! Everybody run for your horses!"

"*Hay-ay! Hay-ay!*" The *Shahiyela* warriors shouted their war cry, waiting in a big band for Two Moon to lead them into battle.

"Warriors, don't run away if the soldiers charge you," he told them. "Stand and fight them. Watch me. I'll stand even if I am sure to be killed!"

It was a brave-up talk to make them strong in their fight. Two Moon led them out at a gallop . . .

After Two Moon's band left to fight Major Reno, a new threat developed from Custer's detachment advancing down Medicine Tail coulee toward the river and the Cheyenne camp.

"They're coming this way!" Bobtail Horse shouted. "Across the ford! We must stop them!"

We saw the soldiers in the coulee were getting closer and closer to the ford, so we trotted out to meet them. An old *Shahiyela* named Mad Wolf, riding a rack-of-bones horse, tried to stop us, saying:

"My sons, do not charge the soldiers. There are too many. Wait until our brothers come back to help!"

He rode along with us a way, whining about how such a small war party would have no chance against a whole army. Finally Bobtail Horse told him:

"Uncle, only Earth and the Heavens last long. If we four can stop the soldiers from capturing our camp, our lives will be well spent.". . .

At this point I interrupted White Cow Bull, suggesting that we try to get closer to the crossing known as Miniconjou Ford. He agreed it would refresh his memory on a few details to go, so I eased the car down a dusty lane between cultivated fields until we reached the river. He sat in silence a long moment before resuming his narrative. Then he spoke in low tones, the Sioux words resonant in the morning quiet:

The Sans Arc and Miniconjou camp circles were back from the ford. We found a low ridge along here and slid off our ponies to take whatever cover we could find. For the first time I saw five Sioux warriors racing down the coulee ahead of the soldiers. They were coming fast and dodging bullets the soldiers were firing at them. Then Bobtail Horse pointed to that bluff beside the ford. On top were three Indians that looked like Crows from their hair style and dress. Bobtail Horse said:

"They are our enemies, guiding the soldiers here."

He fired his muzzleloader at them, then squatted behind the ridge to reload. I fired at them too, for I saw they were shooting at the five Sioux warriors, who were now splashing across the ford at a dead run. My rifle was a repeater, so I kept firing at the Crows until these Sioux were safely on our side of the river. They had no guns, just lances and bows and arrows. But they got off their ponies and joined us behind the ridge. Just then I saw a *Shahiyela* named White Shield, armed with bow and arrows, come riding downriver. He was alone, but we were glad to have another fighting man with us. That made ten of us to defend the ford.

I looked across the ford and saw that the soldiers had stopped at the edge of the river. I had never seen white soldiers before, so I remember thinking how pink and hairy they looked. One white man had little hairs on his face [a mustache] and was wearing a big hat and a buckskin jacket. He was riding a fine-looking big horse, a sorrel with a blazed face and four white stockings. On one side of him was a soldier carrying a flag and riding a gray horse, and on the other was a small man on a dark horse. This small man didn't look much like a white man to me, so I gave the man in the buckskin jacket my attention.* He was looking straight at us across the river. Bobtail Horse told us all to stay hidden so this man couldn't see how few of us there really were.

The man in the buckskin jacket seemed to be the leader of these soldiers, for he shouted something and they all came charging at us across the ford. Bobtail Horse fired first, and I saw a soldier on a gray horse (not the flag carrier) fall out of his saddle into the water. The other soldiers were shooting at us now. The man who seemed to be the soldier chief was firing his heavy rifle fast. I aimed my repeater at him and fired. I saw him fall out of his saddle and hit the water.

Shooting that man stopped the soldiers from charging on. They all reined up their horses and gathered around where he had fallen. I fired again, aiming this time at the soldier with the flag. I saw him go down as another soldier grabbed the flag out of his hands. By this time the air was getting thick with gunsmoke and it was hard to see just what happened. The soldiers were firing again and again, so we were kept busy dodging bullets that kicked up dust all around. When it cleared a little, I saw the soldiers do a strange thing. Some of them got off their

*The "small man" was evidently Mitch Bouyer, half French, half Sioux, who had married into the Crow tribe and served Custer as scout and interpreter for the Crow scouts.

horses in the ford and seemed to be dragging something out of the water, while other soldiers still on horseback kept shooting at us.

Suddenly we heard war cries behind us. I looked back and saw hundreds of Lakotas [Sioux] and *Shahiyela* warriors charging toward us. They must have driven away those other soldiers who had attacked the Hunkpapa camp circle and now were racing to help us drive off these attackers. The soldiers must have seen them too, for they fell back to the far bank of the river, and those still on horseback got off to fight on foot. As warriors rode up to join us at the ridge a big cry went up.

"*Hoka hey!*" the Lakotas were shouting. "They are going!"

I saw this was true. The soldiers were running back up the coulee and swarming out over the higher ground to the north. Bobtail Horse ran to his pony, shouting to us as we caught our ponies.

"Come on! They are running! Hurry!"

He and I led the massed warriors across the ford, for the others knew we had stood bravely to protect the village and willingly followed us.

Another warrior named Yellow Nose, a *Sapawicasa* [Ute] who had been captured as a boy by the *Shahiyela* and had grown up with them, was very brave that day. After we chased the soldiers back from the ford, he galloped out in front of us and got very close to them, then raced back to safety.

I kept riding with the *Shahiyelas*, still hoping that some of them might tell Meotzi later about my courage. We massed for another charge. The *Shahiyela* chief, Comes-in-Sight, and a warrior named Contrary Belly led us that time. The soldiers' horses were so frightened by all the noise we made that they began to bolt in all directions. The soldiers held their fire while they tried to catch their horses. Just then Yellow Nose rushed in again and grabbed a small flag [guidon] from where the soldiers had stuck it in the ground. He carried it off and counted coup [struck blows] on a soldier with its sharp end. He was proving his courage more by counting that coup than if he had killed the soldier.

Now I saw the soldiers were split into two bands, most of them on foot and shooting as they fell back to higher ground, so we made no more mounted charges. I found cover and began shooting at the soldiers. I was a good shot and had one of the few repeating rifles carried by any of our warriors.* It was up to me to use it the best way I could. I kept firing at the two bands of soldiers—first at one, then at the other. It was hard to see through the smoke and dust, but I saw five soldiers go down when I shot at them.

Once in a while some warrior showed his courage by making a charge all by himself. I saw one *Shahiyela*, wearing a spotted war bonnet and a spotted robe of mountain-lion skins, ride out alone.

"He's charging!" someone shouted.

He raced up to the long ridge where the soldiers of one band were making a defense—standing there holding their horses and keeping up a steady fire. This *Shahiyela* charged in almost close enough to touch some of the soldiers and rode around in circles in front of them with bullets kicking up dust all around

him. He came galloping back, and we all cheered him.

"*Ah! Ah!*" he said, meaning "yes" in *Shahiyela*.

Then he unfastened his belt and opened his robe and shook many spent bullets out on the ground . . .

The old man grinned at the memory of such courage.

It was a day of bravery—even for our soldier enemies. They all fought well and died in courage, except for one soldier on a sorrel horse. He broke away from the others and started riding off down the ridge. Two *Shahiyelas* and a Lakota chased after him, shooting at him as they rode. But the soldier's horse was fast and they couldn't catch him. I saw him yank out his revolver and thought he was going to shoot back at these warriors. Instead he put the revolver to his head, pulled the trigger, and fell dead.**

In a little while all my bullets were gone. But by that time the soldiers lay still. We had killed them all. The battle was over. Soon we were shouting victory yells. When the women and children heard us, they came out on the ridge to strip the bodies and catch some of the big horses the soldiers had ridden. Some women had lost husbands or brothers or sons in the fight, so they butchered the soldiers' bodies to show their grief and anger.

I began looking for bullets and weapons in the piles of dead bodies. Near the top of the ridge I saw a naked body and turned it over. The face had little hairs on it and looked like the white man who had worn the buckskin jacket and had fired at me across the ford—the same one I had shot off his horse. I remembered how close some of his bullets had come, so I thought I would take the medicine of his trigger finger to make me an even better shot. Taking out my knife, I began to cut off that finger.

Just then I heard a woman's voice behind me. I turned to see Meotzi and Yellow Bird and an older *Shahiyela* woman standing there. The older woman pointed to the white man's body, saying:

"He is our relative."

Then she signed for me to go away. I looked at Meotzi then and smiled, but she didn't smile back at me, so I wondered if she thought it was wrong for a warrior to be cutting on an enemy's body. I decided she wouldn't be as proud of me if I cut off the white man's finger, and moved away. Pretending to be busy looking for bullets, I glanced back. Meotzi was looking down at the body while the older woman poked her bone sewing awl deep into each of the white man's ears. I heard her say:

"So Long Hair will hear better in the Spirit Land."

That was the first I knew that Long Hair was the soldier chief we had been fighting and the white man I had shot at the ford . . .

The tribes had split up after their victory at Little Bighorn. White Cow Bull never saw Meotzi again after that summer. Perhaps because of her, he never took a wife. After that day in Montana I saw the old man several times at Charlie Thunder Bull's cabin near Oglala, South Dakota, on the Pine Ridge Indian Reservation, making three portraits of him before his death in 1942.

---

*Indian informants agree there were probably not more than a dozen or so repeating rifles in working order in the entire village, although more were captured as the battle progressed.

**This may have been 2nd Lieutenant Henry M. Harrington, C Company, whose body was never identified.

## JOSEPH WHITE BULL

One of my proudest possessions is an old single-trail war bonnet, mounted entirely on elk leather, which belonged to Sitting Bull's "fighting nephew," Chief Joseph White Bull. I have documentation that he wore the headdress during the Battle of the Little Bighorn.

I first met the Chief, then a grizzled old veteran of nearly ninety, in the mid-1930's. Since he spoke no English, all our many conferences were carried on in Sioux and sign language. My most memorable meeting with him took place in 1939 at his log house in the Indian settlement at Cherry Creek, on the Cheyenne River Indian Reservation in South Dakota.

Throughout most of his lifetime White Bull was, without doubt, the most illustrious warrior of the entire Sioux nation. Twenty-six years old at the time of the Custer fight in 1876, he had already taken part in nineteen battles, raids, and skirmishes—ten against white men, one against government Indian scouts, the others against Indian enemies. His first notable engagement was in the Fetterman fight in 1866. Prior to the Battle of the Little Bighorn, he had counted seven coups (six of them "firsts"), killed three enemies, wounded another, taken two scalps, shot three enemy horses, rescued six wounded comrades, recovered a dead body under enemy fire, captured forty-five enemy horses, and been hit twice by enemy bullets. At least one horse had been shot from under him in battle. He meticulously kept this "honor count" in an old ledger, which he eagerly showed me.

Page after page of this personal military history was illustrated with White Bull's own colored drawings, executed in the old Indian style and much like those formerly painted on hides.

He was a powerfully built old fellow, conveying even in later life an impression of great physical strength and stamina. His hair, gathered in loose tresses at the ear lobes, was nearly white. His prominent nose sprawled slightly leftward as though it had been broken. His most arresting feature, however, was his intense, almost animallike expression of fierce pride; and his eyes, while showing signs of milky blue in the pupils (as often occurs among Indians of advanced age), were alert and piercing. He had a haunting habit of chuckling, even laughing, when recounting the more gory details of his sanguinary career:

I am the only one left of eight scalp-shirt men [head chiefs] of the Miniconjou tribe. My father was Makes-Room, hereditary chief of my tribe. My mother was Good Feather Woman, sister of Sitting Bull, so the great chief was my uncle.

My original name given me in boyhood was Bull-Standing-With-Cow. After my first fight against government Indian scouts in the Powder River country, when I was fifteen years old, I was given my grandfather's name, White Bull, by another uncle named Black Moon. . . .

At the Little Bighorn, White Bull, armed with a seventeen-shot Winchester, fought first against Reno's force and then rode off to join the battle against Custer:

Little bunches of Lakotas and Cheyennes were riding into the ravine. I rode up to where two Lakotas and two Cheyennes were sitting their horses, waiting to charge the soldiers. I shouted to them:

"Only Heaven and Earth last long!"

I rode past them up the ravine. They took courage and followed me. We were behind the soldiers as we got up on the ridge, and we began to shoot at them. Some of them got off their horses and hid behind them to shoot back at us.

Lakotas were riding all around, shooting at the soldiers, who didn't go any farther along the ridge. I rode around the ridge and dodged the bullets until I met a party of warriors with Crazy Horse. He was a chief of the Oglala and a brave fighter. He wore plain white buckskins and let his hair hang loose with no feathers in it. He had white spots painted here and there on his face for protection in battle, and it was said he was bulletproof.

The soldiers were divided into two bunches. I galloped my pony in between the two bunches and kept close to his neck until I rode clear around one of the bunches and circled back to Crazy Horse. I shouted to him:

"*Hoka hey*, brother! This life will not last forever!"

I started to circle the soldiers again. This time Crazy Horse and the others followed. Some of the soldiers ran like scared rabbits, and we rode after them. One soldier was riding a black horse. A Lakota on foot shot him, and he fell off the horse. I ran up to strike him with my quirt.

One of the soldiers blew on a bugle. The others began to get on their horses. I dared Crazy Horse to lead a charge against them. He refused, so I rode out alone and came up behind a soldier on a bay horse. I grabbed his coat and pulled him out of his saddle. He tried to shoot me, but his rifle fired into the air; he fell screaming to the ground. I rode down two soldiers and lashed them with my quirt. Crazy Horse struck both of these men after I did.

The soldiers who were still alive got off their horses and lay down to shoot. I charged through them twice. They were firing up in the air and acted as though they were drunk. A brave Lakota rode up and chased away their horses. Soon bays and sorrels and grays were running everywhere. Many Lakotas stopped shooting and began to chase these loose horses. I caught a sorrel horse. Just after that my pony went down with bullets in his shoulder and ribs. So I had to fight on foot.

One soldier fired his rifle at me, then threw it at my head. He tried to wrestle with me. I had a bad time keeping him from getting my rifle. He began hitting me on the face. Then he grabbed my long hair in his hands and tried to bite my nose off!

White Bull laughed, stroking his nose.

Two Lakotas came running up and began hitting this soldier with their war clubs. He let go of me. I knocked him down with the butt of my rifle. He was a brave man and put up a good fight—except that he tried to bite off my nose.

Not many soldiers were left alive by this time. We surrounded them and kept shooting them down. They acted like drunk people. Some of them shot wildly into the air, not hitting any of us. The Army was crazy to have sent such a small band of soldiers against us, anyway. They could never have beaten us in that fight.

One soldier still alive toward the last wore a buckskin coat with fringes on it. I thought this man was leader of the soldiers, because he had ridden ahead of all the others as they came along the ridge. He saw me now and shot at me twice with his revolver, missing me both times. I raised my rifle and fired at him; he went down. Then I saw another soldier crawl over to him. The leader was dead.

By the middle of the afternoon all the soldiers were dead. The fight lasted only a short time.* All of us were crazy. We had killed many soldiers. They had attacked us and meant to wipe us out. We were fighting for our lives and homeland. Cries of victory went up. Our women came through the timber by the river and began to strip the dead soldiers.

Some of the sisters and wives and mothers of slain warriors cut the bodies of the soldiers to pieces. They were crazy with sorrow. Two old women took the clothes off a wounded soldier, who pretended to be dead. When he was naked, one of the women started to cut off something he had. He jumped up and tried to fight the women. One of them tried to stab him with her knife while he was trying to get away from the other one. Then a third woman came up and stabbed the soldier. [The old man laughed.] He really died that time!

Some of the Lakotas said they found whiskey bottles on the soldiers after the fight.** The soldiers had acted like drunk people.

My cousin Bad Soup [Bad Juice] was stripping the soldier I thought had been the leader and held up the buckskin coat. He looked in the pockets of the coat and brought out some papers with pictures on them [maps]. In one of the pockets he found coils of long yellow hair. But the dead leader had his hair cut short.

"*Onhey!*" Bad Soup cried. "That man there was Long Hair Custer. He thought he was the greatest man on earth, but he lies there now. And he cut his hair so he would not be scalped!"

He was the leader who had tried to kill me. But I had killed him . . .

The old man looked both relieved and vaguely troubled. After several moments he said: "I never told this to anyone before. I was afraid the white men would hang me or lock me up for a long time, if they knew I had killed Long Hair. *Hecetuyelo*. So be it."***

In the Custer fight alone White Bull had counted seven coups, killed two soldiers in hand-to-hand fighting, and captured two guns and twelve horses. Before leaving the field, he took two pairs of trousers from dead troopers, which he later presented to his father. All told, it was an enviable record of reckless courage—probably unexceeded by any other Sioux or Cheyenne warrior at the Little Bighorn.

White Bull and other leaders decided not to follow Sitting Bull and other Sioux into "Grandmother's Land" (Canada, ruled, of course, by Victoria, R.I.). Instead, the Miniconjou surrendered to white military authorities and became "agency Indians" at Cheyenne River.

His last big adventure occurred in his fifty-seventh year, when, almost single-handedly, he "captured" several hundred White River Utes who had jumped reservation in Utah and were crossing Wyoming to reach the Sioux country in South Dakota. Only an Indian leader of White Bull's reputation could have dissuaded these Utes from making considerable trouble, and, as it turned out, they meekly submitted to his authority. He eventually led them to his home reservation, where they stayed about a year before the government returned them to Utah. In the meantime White Bull married one of their women, a marriage that lasted as long as the Utes' temporary exile. (He had fifteen wives in all.)

White Bull died in 1947, aged ninety-seven. I like to think he'd be pleased to know how dearly I treasure his old war bonnet.

*Lacking clocks or watches, Indians then told time by the sun's position. All Indian informants agreed that the action against Custer's command on the ridge occupied the time it took for the sun to travel the width of the shadow of a tepee pole across the ground. By actual measurement this turned out to be almost exactly twenty minutes.

**Troopers carried rations of whiskey in their canteens, but probably lacked enough to get hard-drinking troopers intoxicated.

***White Bull apparently told the late Stanley Vestal much the same story. See Vestal's article, "The Man Who Killed Custer," in AMERICAN HERITAGE, February, 1957.

## DEWEY BEARD

I first heard of Dewey Beard in 1935 on the Pine Ridge Reservation. Assured that he had participated in the fight against Custer, I also learned that he had taken part in other Indian-white conflicts, including the massacre at Wounded Knee in 1890—climax of the Ghost Dance activities.

Tracking down Beard—better known locally by his Sioux name *Wasu Maza*, meaning "Iron Hail"—led me first to his isolated one-room log house in the Potato Creek district, many miles northeast of the agency. The place was deserted. His Indian neighbors told me the old man and his aging wife, Alice, spent the summer months in the nearby South Dakota Bad Lands. I found the couple camped in a canvas tepee near a craggy defile called Cedar Pass. This out-of-the-way location, I soon discovered, had more than casual meaning for Beard. Following an old Indian trail through this pass, hundreds of Ghost Dancers from the Cheyenne River country to the north had fled south to their rendezvous with destiny at Wounded Knee. Beard had been one of them and had narrowly missed sharing their fate.

Dressed in yellowish buckskins and wearing an ermine-trimmed war bonnet, Dewey Beard was an imposing figure. At seventy-eight that first meeting, he stood tall and lodgepole straight, his proud head held high, his jutting jaw housing a full set of his own teeth, which remained white and even until his dying day. He wore his

long black hair in two loose hanks. In the thirties and forties many old-time Sioux continued to favor long hair as a means of gaining or retaining spiritual power, but Beard had a special and rather surprising reason for wearing long hair.

"I let my hair grow this way," he explained solemnly in Sioux, for he spoke no English, "because our Saviour, Jesus Christ, is always pictured with long hair."

The old man's regal appearance was an immediate challenge for my pencils, pastels, and paints. The sketch I made of him that evening at Cedar Pass was the first of many portraits I painted of Beard. Sometimes I portrayed him in full regalia. More often, though, I depicted him as I later usually saw him—in drab, cast-off garments given to him by well-meaning missionaries. Even dressed as a grotesque old scarecrow, he never failed to convey a majestic sense of nobility that set him apart from his own tribesmen. My sketch completed, we talked late into the night. I asked him if he remembered the day Long Hair Custer fell.

"Yes, I remember well," he said, a glint of excitement in his old dark eyes. "None of us who were there could forget. I was almost eighteen that summer. Never before or since that time did my people gather in such great numbers. Our camp on the Greasy Grass [Little Bighorn] stretched four miles along the river—six great camp circles, each a half mile across, with thousands of Lakota fighting men and their families."

"How many thousands?" I wanted to know. "Can you say?"

Beard signed No with a wave of a bony brown hand. He grinned, adding:

In that long-ago time none of my people knew more than a thousand numbers. We believed no honest man needed to know more than that many. There was my own tribe, the Miniconjou. There were our cousins, the Hunkpapa, the Sans Arc, the Two Kettles, the Sihasapa [Blackfoot Sioux], the Brulé, and the Oglala—all our Seven Council Fires. There were many of our eastern relatives, too—the Yankton and the Santee. And our kinsmen from the north were there—the Yanktonai and the Assiniboin. Our friends and allies the Cheyenne were there in force, and with them were smaller bands of Arapaho and Gros Ventre. It was a great village and we had great leaders.

He paused, lending emphasis to what for him was talk of giants.

Hump, Fast Bull, and High Backbone led my tribe. Crazy Horse headed the Oglala. *Inkpaduta* [Scarlet Tip] led the Santee. Lame White Man and Ice Bear led the Cheyenne. But the greatest leader of all was the chief of the Hunkpapa—Sitting Bull. As long as we were all camped together, we looked on him as head chief. We all rallied around him because he stood for our old way of life and the freedom we had always known. We were not there to make war, but, if need be, we were ready to fight for our sacred rights. Since the white man's government had promised our leaders that we could wander and hunt in our old territory as long as the grass should grow, we did not believe the white soldiers had any business in our hunting grounds. Yet they came to attack us anyway.

I slept late the morning of the fight. The day before, I had been hunting buffalo and I had to ride far to find the herds because there were so many people in the valley. I came back with meat, but I was very tired. So when I got up, the camp women were already starting out to dig for wild turnips. Two of my uncles had left early for another buffalo hunt. Only my grandmother and a third uncle were in the tepee, and the sun was high overhead and hot. I walked to the river to take a cool swim, then got hungry and returned to the tepee at dinner time [noon].

"When you finish eating," my uncle said, "go to our horses. Something might happen today. I feel it in the air."

I hurried to Muskrat Creek and joined my younger brother, who was herding the family horses. By the time I reached the herd, I heard shouting in the village. People were yelling that white soldiers were riding toward the camp.

I climbed Black Butte for a look around the country. I saw a long column of soldiers coming and a large party of Hunkpapa warriors, led by Sitting Bull's nephew, One Bull, riding out to meet them. I could see One Bull's hand raised in the peace sign to show the soldiers that our leaders only wanted to talk them into going away and leaving us alone. But all at once the soldiers spread out for attack and began to fire, and the fight was on. I caught my favorite war pony, a small buckskin mustang I called *Sunkawakan Zi Chischila* [Little Yellow Horse] and raced him back to camp to get ready for battle.

I had no time to paint *Zi Chischila* properly for making war, just a minute or so to braid his tail and to daub a few white hail spots of paint on my own forehead for protection before I galloped out on the little buckskin to help defend the camp. I met four other Lakotas riding fast. Three were veteran fighters, armed with rifles; the other was young like me and carried a bow and arrows as I did. One of the veterans went down. I saw my chance to act bravely and filled the gap. We all turned when we heard shooting at the far side of the village nearest the Miniconjou camp circle and rode fast to meet this new danger. I could see swirls of dust and hear shooting on the hills and bluffs across the river. Hundreds of other warriors joined us as we splashed across the ford near our camp and raced up the hills to charge into the thickest of the fighting.

This new battle was a turmoil of dust and warriors and soldiers, with bullets whining and arrows hissing all around. Sometimes a bugle would sound and the shooting would get louder. Some of the soldiers were firing pistols at close range. Our knives and war clubs flashed in the sun. I could hear bullets whiz past my ears. But I kept going and shouting, "It's a good day to die!" so that everyone who heard would know I was not afraid of being killed in battle.

Then a Lakota named Spotted Rabbit rode unarmed among us, calling out a challenge to all the warriors to join him. He shouted, "Let's take their leader alive!" I had no thought of what we would do with this leader once we caught him; it was a daring feat that required more courage and much more skill than killing him. I dug my heels into my pony's flanks to urge

him on faster to take part in the capture.

A tall white man in buckskins kept shouting at the soldiers and looked to be their leader. Following Spotted Rabbit, I charged toward this leader in buckskins. We were almost on top of him when Spotted Rabbit's pony was shot from under him. *Zi Chischila* shied to one side, and it was too late. A Miniconjou named Charging Hawk rushed in and shot the leader at close range. In a little while all the soldiers were dead. The battle was over.

The soldier chief we had tried to capture lay on the ground with the reins of his horse's bridle tied to his wrist. It was a fine animal, a blaze-faced sorrel with four white stockings. A Santee named Walks-Under-the-Ground took that horse.* Then he told everyone that the leader lying there dead was Long Hair; so that was the first I knew who we had been fighting. I thought it was a strange name for a soldier chief who had his hair cut short.

Our attempt to save Long Hair's life had failed. But we all felt good about our victory over the soldiers and celebrated with a big scalp dance. But our triumph was hollow. A winter or so later more soldiers came to round us up on reservations. There were too many of them to fight now. We were split up into bands and no longer felt strong. At last we were ready for peace and believed we would have no more trouble.

Beard tried to settle down and raise a family with Chief Big Foot's band of Miniconjous on the Cheyenne River. The old life was nearly over. White hide-hunters almost finished off the buffalo herds in the 1880's. Attempting to follow the white man's road, the Sioux did not take kindly to reservation life. Times were hard, and government beef rations were far from sufficient to sustain the Indians.

In 1890 many Sioux, including Big Foot's people, eagerly began to practice the Ghost Dance. Desperate and starving, they believed that worship of an Indian messiah would rescue the red race from the white man's hated civilization and restore the vanished buffalo. As avid a believer as any of his tribesmen, Beard was convinced that his departed ancestors would return from beyond the grave to share in a great revival of Sioux culture if he performed the Ghost Dance often and fervently enough.

Neither Beard nor more than a handful of his tribe actually wanted war with the whites, who, by the winter of 1890, were fearful that the Ghost Dance would lead to an armed intertribal outbreak. Troops were called out to surround the Sioux reservations. Big Foot tried to calm his followers, often telling them:

"I will stand in peace until my last day!"

When military pressure mounted, the old Chief grew panicky. Knowing that vast numbers of Ghost Dancers were gathering in the vicinity of Pine Ridge Agency, Big Foot and his band jumped the reservation and fled south through the Bad Lands to seek whatever sanctuary they

*Sometimes more properly translated as "Sounds-the-Ground-as-He-Walks," this was a son of *Inkpaduta*.

could find. Soldiers were hard on their heels, but they eluded them until they reached Porcupine Butte on Pine Ridge Reservation, where they encountered Long Hair Custer's old 7th Cavalry. Big Foot promptly surrendered; he was too sick and old to resist. He and his band were escorted to Wounded Knee Creek to camp for the night.

Beard said sadly:

That is another time I will never forget. It was the last night on earth for my first wife and family. Next morning the soldiers surrounded us and ordered us to give up our weapons. They even took away our skinning knives. But we were not looking for war and wanted to do as the soldiers ordered.

One Indian's gun was fired by accident. I heard later it belonged to Sitting Bull's deaf-mute son, who couldn't hear the order to disarm. After that shot, the soldiers let loose with everything they had. Unarmed, we didn't have a chance. Men, women, children, even babies, were shot down. Soldiers galloped after those who ran and cut them down with sabers. Then they opened up on us with cannons [Hotchkiss guns] and pounded everything flat—tepees, people, even horses and dogs. I was struck by bullets in my arm, chest, and leg, but I ran limping down a gully and got away.

Hiding in a cutbank, I looked back at the camp. My wife and child were lying there motionless. A few paces away were my old mother and father, my sister, and, beyond them, my two younger brothers. All of them were dead. I waited there in the snow beside the cutbank and prayed for death . . .

Only a handful of Miniconjous were fortunate enough to survive. Shouting "Remember Little Bighorn!" troopers of the 7th reaped a whirlwind revenge for Custer's 1876 defeat. Nearly three hundred* Indians were slaughtered at Wounded Knee—among them the entire family of a warrior who, according to his own account, had tried to save Custer's life.

For a time Beard thought only of vengeance on the whites. He knew of places in the Bad Lands from which he might wage an embittered, lone-hand vendetta against the soldier enemies. But happily, Beard's one-man war against the United States Army never materialized.

The turning point came when General Nelson A. Miles took command of the military and sought justice through the prosecution of those 7th Cavalry officers responsible for the Wounded Knee tragedy. Beard's testimony as a survivor of the massacre was considered by Miles to be vital to a War Department prosecution. Little actually resulted from the investigation, however. Instead, Congress awarded twenty-nine Medals of Honor to soldiers who had participated in this last campaign against the Sioux—*twenty-three* specifically for action at Wounded Knee!

Nevertheless, Beard and Miles became fast friends. Through the General, Beard met other high officials. After the turn of the century Miles summoned Beard to

Washington and introduced him to Admiral George Dewey, fresh from Manila Bay and the Spanish-American War. Beard later took the naval hero's surname, adding it to his old Sioux nickname, to become "Dewey Beard."

While in Washington, Beard was asked by the sculptor James Earle Fraser to pose for a bas-relief profile on a proposed new coin. When the buffalo nickel was issued in 1913, the noble Indian profile turned out to be a composite, and Beard was never sure which part of it was patterned after his own features.**

Back in Sioux country Beard remarried. For a half century Dewey and Alice Beard were harmonious fixtures in the South Dakota Sioux community. Old resentments faded. Beard's prominence among Indians and white historians grew as he became one of a dwindling group of aging warriors who had been wounded in battle and were thus entitled to perform with honor the Wounded Warrior Dance. Moreover, he was one of the remaining few who had fought Custer.

I knew him well in his winter years. During a visit in the early fifties, I asked him if he had indeed been able to forgive the soldiers who had wounded him and had slain his family.

"I am sorry for all that happened at Wounded Knee," he said, combing his bony fingers through hair still black and glossy. "But now my heart is full and warm with friendship for the white man."

Beard proved it when his grown son Tommy, his only living offspring, died of the "white man's sickness"—tuberculosis. I tried to help him through his heartbreak. Turning briefly from his sorrow, the old fellow named me his son to take his beloved Tommy's place—an honor I gratefully accepted.

When my wife Jan and I were married in Rapid City, South Dakota, in July, 1954, none of our parents, hers or mine, were able to be with us. Filling the gap, Dewey and Alice came forward to shake our hands and wish us well. Beard had a folded cloth under one arm. As he shook it free, I saw it was an old-time courting blanket—brilliant red and green with a beaded strip dividing the colors—which I knew Alice had painstakingly made. He silently draped it, first around my shoulder, then Jan's, encircling us together in the Sioux fashion of marriage. Then, speaking our Sioux names, he told us we were "one, now and always."

With the death of Sitting Bull's deaf-mute son, John, in May, 1955, Beard became the last survivor—Indian or white—of Custer's Last Stand at Little Bighorn. He died the following November, the final, grand old patriarch of the fighting Sioux.

*The Army officially set the number of dead at thirty-one troopers and 128 Indians.

**Fraser's aboriginal models for the buffalo nickel also included Chief Iron Tail of Buffalo Bill's Wild West show, an Oglala, and Two Guns White Calf, a Montana Piegan. Fraser's memoirs of his early life appeared in AMERICAN HERITAGE, December, 1968.

# EPILOGUE *By* ROBERT M. UTLEY

## Twenty years after the Little Bighorn— what happened to a fighting people

Only seven years after the last spasm at Wounded Knee, a white storekeeper named James Freeman from Mount Pleasant, Michigan, a financial casualty of the Panic of 1893, got a job with the U.S. Indian Service at Pine Ridge, South Dakota. There, as a hobby, he took up photography and recorded the life of a people in the throes of cultural transition.

The Great Sioux Reservation—all of present South Dakota west of the Missouri River—had been set aside for the seven tribes of Teton Sioux by the Treaty of 1868. Pine Ridge Agency, established in 1878, was where the Oglala were driven after Custer's defeat.

The decade of the 1880's was a traumatic and tempestuous time for the Pine Ridge Sioux. The reservation had been cut down by the Black Hills cession of 1877 and again in 1890, when the Tetons surrendered nine million acres and accepted six separate reservations in place of the single large one. Using control of rations as a lever, Indian agents sought to destroy the old system of government, the old religion, the old social customs, the old dress and hair styles—all, in short, that gave stability, continuity, and meaning to life. Instead of nomadic warrior-huntsmen following the buffalo, living in skin tepees, and worshipping deities associated with nature, the Sioux were to become sedentary Christian farmers. Rent by quarrelling factions, precariously ruled by the agent and his Indian police force, the Oglala dreamed of their past freedom. Most, refusing to recognize the finality of their conquest, resisted the "reforms" being forced on them.

Spreading over the Sioux reservations in 1889–90, the Ghost Dance religion seemed to offer a road back into the past, only to be shattered on the bloody field of Wounded Knee, eighteen miles east of Pine Ridge Agency. That tragedy accomplished what a decade of "civilization" programs had not: it broke the spirit of all the Teton Sioux tribes.

The life that James Freeman photographed in 1898 was thus, in the externals his cameras caught, a grotesque mixture of what the Sioux had been and what their white rulers wanted them to become. Shortly after taking these pictures, Freeman left Pine Ridge and ultimately returned to Mount Pleasant to live out a long and useful life. His photographs found their way into the collections of the Clarke Historical Library of Central Michigan University in Mount Pleasant, where they now offer a fascinating record of a proud people in the early stages of cultural transformation.

*Mr. Utley, author of several books about Indians and the frontier, is chief historian of the National Park Service and former president of the Western History Association.*

*The boy above, in his Fauntleroy costume, would only recently have been happier in breechcloth and moccasins, and similarly changed are the onlookers below. The annual summer sun dance had been prohibited by the Indian Bureau in the late 1890's as something barbarous and heathenish. Freeman's picture shows the Fourth of July celebration, which now provided a pallid substitute. A mock attack on the village was followed by horse races, dances, a feast, and other ceremonies pleasing to the paleface.*

While Indian social and political institutions disintegrated, the girls of the Pine Ridge Sioux began to learn to be housewives (top, left) and the women below, as befitted members of an Indian policeman's family, dressed in Mother Hubbards. Grandmother, seated in front of them, clings to her Sioux heritage and costume. Observe here, incidentally, the white man's wagons and equipment. The woman above has kept her traditional garb but adopted an iron bedstead, bureau, lamp, and alarm clock.

# Picnics Long Ago

*If it rained, the painters failed to record it*

Food tastes better outdoors, and it always has. Nowadays this rule, which every child learns early in life, can be seen in operation at tailgate parties at football games or wherever spectator sports are in season. You can see it under more elegant circumstances throughout American history, beginning with the Pilgrims' first alfresco party for the Indians. It reached some sort of apogee in the nineteenth century, in the period brought back to us so hauntingly in the writings of Washington Irving and on the canvases of the painters of the Hudson River school.

The picnickers of the last century were overdressed by our standards, but the spirit of conviviality was there, the landscape was unscarred by civilization, the breezes were sweet smelling, and the vistas were infinitely clear. Wicker baskets slung over their arms, they would search for a pleasant clearing to feast on cold meats, hard-boiled eggs, jars of preserves, wine, bread, fruit. Afterward someone might strum a guitar or put a bow to a violin, young couples would wander away for privacy, and children would rollick about. As Irving wrote to his sister in 1840:

We have picnic parties . . . sometimes in some inland valley or piece of wood, sometimes on the banks of the Hudson, where some repair by land, and others by water.

*Left: The setting for Thomas P. Rossitter's* A Picnic on the Hudson, 1868, *was undoubtedly near West Point. The party included General Truman Seymour (seated, far left); white-bearded George Pope Morris, author of "Woodman, Spare That Tree!" and Robert Parrott (standing, far right), the gun inventor. Above: Less formal citizenry appear in Jerome B. Thompson's* The Picnick.

*The stillness of a summer afternoon suffuses* The Picnic, *which was painted near Mount Mansfield, Vermont, in the mid-nineteenth century by the genre artist Jerome B. Thompson.*

You would be delighted with these picturesque assemblages, on some wild woodland point jutting into the Tappan Sea, with gay groups on the grass under the trees; carriages glistening through the woods; a yacht with flapping sails and fluttering streamers anchored about half a mile from shore, and rowboats plying to and from it, filled with lady passengers. . . .

Charles Dickens wrote with the same spirit when, on his first visit to the United States in 1842, he joined a party travelling from St. Louis to see the Looking Glass Prairie, on the eastern side of the Mississippi River, in Illinois. Named apparently for the way its tall, shimmering grasses reflected the sun and the sky, Looking Glass Prairie was a hard, nearly thirty-mile trip from St. Louis. As the Englishman wrote in his *American Notes:*

We encamped near a solitary log-house, for the sake of its water, and dined upon the plain. The baskets contained roast fowls, buffalo's tongue (an exquisite dainty, by-the-way), ham,

bread, cheese, and butter; biscuits, champagne, sherry; lemons and sugar for punch; and abundance of rough ice. The meal was delicious, and the entertainers were the soul of kindness and good humour. I have often recalled that cheerful party to my pleasant recollection since, and shall not easily forget, in junketings nearer home with friends of older date, my boon companions on the Prairie.

We know that other writers on picnics found the same camaraderie that Irving and Dickens did. Thoreau joined Emerson on such outings from Concord, Massachusetts, and Hawthorne and Melville began their long friendship on a picnic-expedition in the Berkshires in 1850. Of course, nature being untrustworthy, there were times when rain interrupted the rites. Hawthorne and Melville, for example, were forced to seek cover from a thundershower on their climb to the top of Monument Mountain. And a young friend of the Irving family,

*As shadows lengthen, one couple begins cleaning up as others listen to a guitar player (they were popular in those days, too) in Thomas Cole's serene* The Pic-Nic, *1844.*

Angelica Hamilton of Nevis (now Irvington), New York, recorded a similar incident in 1843 in a letter to her brother Alexander, grandson of our first Secretary of the Treasury. Young Alexander was then serving with Irving at the American Legation in Madrid. The letter, now at Sleepy Hollow Restorations, Tarrytown, New York, reads in part:

Mary [another sister] has told you of our visit to Sandy Hook, since then one Picnic has come off in a most pelting rain, highly ludicrous. We had appointed the day some time before, invited the Minturns, prepared the baskets, & accordingly though the clouds looked lowering set sail without any wind & drifted up to silver brook. When there we thought it was best to try for the inmates of the cottage, so Bow was deputed a committee of sixteen & succeeded in bringing off two Miss Irvings & Mrs. Romeyn with a small but choice addition to the repast, the best loaf of bread in the world; we then crossed over [the Hudson] to try & get the Hoffmans . . . but in vain. By this time the cooks commenced opperations, Pa & Minturn. We had a capital dinner & a great deal of fun when in the midst of all; down came the rain in torrents. The cabin became warm, the sky light had to be taken off to admit the air, & the water of course followed. We laughed a great deal notwithstanding, for the angelic Mrs. Minturn is very funny on such occasions, & he is truly a good fellow & full of interest & information upon every thing that is going on, so it ended in our all coming ashore at the cottage & Pa's sending the carriage down for us; their going home immediately, & the Irvings passing the night with Mrs. Minturn.

Artists like those represented on these pages captured these moments of genteel good fellowship on canvas, affording us a glimpse of our forefathers at their informal best, in settings that make us catch our breath for their beauty. We must travel too far nowadays to find a spot that is secluded or a view that is uninterrupted. The paintings here serve as a pleasant reminder of what once was.

*—The Editors*

*Dusk is in the offing, and the weary picnickers in Jerome B. Thompson's* Belated Party on Mansfield Mountain, *1858, face a long hike home.*

*The painting, a detail of which is reproduced here, was discovered in 1969 by a carpenter while tearing down a barn outside Philadelphia.*

# SPHAIRISTIKÉ,

*Introduced not quite a century ago*

*under a name born for oblivion, the game*

*itself promises to last forever*

# ANYONE?

*By* E. M. HALLIDAY

Miss Mary Ewing Outerbridge was unquestionably one of New York's most respectable young ladies. Her Staten Island family was socially impeccable and correspondingly well-to-do; she was seen in the best places at the right times. It was therefore a considerable shock when the attractive Miss Outerbridge, returning from a holiday in Bermuda in March, 1874, had trouble getting through customs in New York.

Certainly she looked like anything but a smuggler, but in her luggage the inspectors found some curious and unidentifiable objects. There was a long, narrow net that did not seem to be designed for catching fish; there were several implements with long handles and webbed heads. Were they rug beaters? Snowshoes? Butterfly catchers?

Miss Outerbridge explained that these things were the equipment for a new outdoor game called sphairistiké. This was Greek to the inspectors, and it was only because the young lady's brother, who was travelling with her, had connections in the shipping business that they were persuaded to pass her without further ado.

RAPHO-GUILLUMETTE

49

*Major Walter Clopton Wingfield, the father of lawn tennis, posing in a costume that would have shocked the court set a generation later.*

A few weeks later, passengers on boats sailing past the grounds of the Staten Island Cricket and Baseball Club were puzzled to observe a game being played on the fresh spring grass that was clearly neither cricket nor baseball. Across a net hung between two posts, gentlemen and— yes, ladies!—were hitting a bouncing rubber ball with some sort of bat, running hither and thither with little cries of exhilaration.

Tennis had come to America.

The immigration of what is today one of America's favorite warm-weather sports occurred almost simultaneously with its birth. It was only in February, 1874, that Major Walter C. Wingfield, a British officer and sportsman, had applied for a patent on "a new and improved portable court for playing the ancient game of tennis." The truth was—and Major Wingfield claimed as much —that the new "portable court" constituted a new game. The "ancient game," which was and is called court ten-

*Six years after Miss Outerbridge imported the game, an artist-journalist gave this impression of a tournament on Staten Island, 1880.*

nis, is an indoor affair with complicated rules deriving from the fact that the ball can bounce off all four walls plus the ceiling and still be in play. It goes back some five hundred years, and there are familiar allusions to it in Shakespeare. Major Wingfield's game, which he first introduced to liven up a house party in Wales in 1873, was far simpler. All it required was a level expanse of lawn, a couple of posts and a net, and rackets to hit the ball with. It was, in short, much like badminton, which also appeared about 1873, with the important difference that in lawn tennis a rubber ball was used instead of a feathered "bird." This made for a more energetic contest, which was what the major was after.

It is a tribute to the intrinsic appeal of tennis that it caught on despite the name with which Major Wingfield first encumbered it. A classical scholar to the extent that became a gentleman, he based its name, sphairistiké, on a Greek word that means "ball-playing." Arcane nomenclature may have helped convince the proper authorities that he had something patentable, but for a popular game this was, as various wits remarked, a bit sticky. "I hear," wrote one, "that Major Wingfield . . . intends bringing out an indoor game at Christmas with a Latin name. . . . The name, I understand, will not exceed ten syllables, and may be easily mastered in six lessons." Incidentally, badminton took its name from Badminton Manor, where the game was first played in England. As the major's family were the possessors of Wingfield Manor, it may have been by a narrow miss that tennis was not christened wingfield. In any event, since the new game was clearly descended from court tennis, the nickname lawn tennis was quickly taken up, and sphairistiké soon forgotten.

One thing that did seem to be a kind of subliminal tribute to Major Wingfield's family name was the shape of his original court, for it was in fact wing-shaped—that is, narrow at the net and wide at the two base lines. There was no evident advantage to this. The net was high and sagging, ranging from seven feet at the posts to four feet eight inches at the middle. Since the court was just sixty feet long, it is obvious that the only way to get a ball over the net and still keep it within the lines was to pop it up in a gentle parabola. Even at the net's low point anything distantly related to a drive carried the ball across the base line and out. It is thus not surprising that lawn tennis at first was looked upon as something of a lady's game, or at best a diversion for mixed company that would not derange a lady's costume or composure. Its evolution into the fast and gruelling competition that is seen at any modern championship match was, however, rather rapid.

By the time the first All-England championship matches were held at Wimbledon in 1877, the court had become a sensible rectangle with the same dimensions it has to-

*Early problems: artists who misunderstood the game; sartorial efforts to put mixed doubles on an equal-rights basis; impromptu court sites better adapted for cattle grazing than ball bouncing.*

OVERLEAF: *Although we have been unable to find a photograph of Mary Outerbridge, she is with us here, for she took this picture of the Staten Island Cricket Club tennis courts in 1880. Her friend Alice Austen, today famous for her photography, watches critically from the service line of the third court over, right side.*

day: seventy-eight by twenty-seven feet for the singles game. The net was now down to five feet at the posts and three feet three inches in the middle. These changes apparently were arrived at by judicious trial and copious error, the end in view being always a livelier game.

Sphairistiké, as played by Major Wingfield and his cronies, was scored like badminton, points accruing only to the server and counting one each up to the winning total of fifteen or twenty-one. But there was something about the game—its ambiance of green lawns, pretty ladies in long dresses, gentlemen in sports jackets, tea and lemonade—that made the old court-tennis scoring system more attractive. The first point scored counted fifteen; the next made thirty; then forty; then game. If you got no points, your score was "love"; if you tied the score at forty-all it was "deuce"; after that you had to make two points to win—advantage and game. The origin of this dreamy terminology is lost in the mists of time, but there are rival schools of thought, particularly about "love." A favorite theory holds that this is an anglicization of the French *l'oeuf*, an egg of course being equivalent to zero; another theory sees "love" as meaning "nothing" in the sense of, "She did it for love, not money." (Shakespeare may have been of this camp: note *Much Ado About Nothing*, which is about love.) Etymology unfortunately offers little support to either speculation, but whatever its genesis, the romantic scoring system has persisted, with its somewhat dubious logic, since its official adoption in 1877.

In America, as in England, tennis remained for its first quarter century largely a game for the affluent and elegant few. A suitably fine lawn was not likely to be found except on a private estate or on the grounds of an exclusive club. Only four people could play at one time, moreover—although it seems that a few bold and brief experiments were made with three or four on each side. The Outerbridges' Staten Island club soon became a leading center for the game, as did clubs in Newport, Rhode Island, and Philadelphia, both of which had courts as early as 1876. A distressing lack of uniformity with regard to courts, nets, and balls led to the establishment of the United States National Lawn Tennis Association in 1881—still the national arbiter of the game today, although the word *national* has since been dropped from the title.

Newport, in the 1880's and 90's, was the most fashionable summer resort in America, with the consequence

*In its first decades tennis was mostly for the leisured and affluent—the sort of people who posed for this memento of the Toledo, Ohio, Outing Club about 1885. The tennis players in their casually formal dress, the high-rise bicycles, the punch bowl and the waiters, the charmingly nonfunctional vagaries of the building itself—all bespeak a long-lost time when life was more relaxed.*

that the national championship tennis matches were played there from 1881 until 1915, when they were moved to the more accessible West Side Tennis Club at Forest Hills, New York. At Newport's famous Casino, play on the beautiful grass courts was usually not taken too seriously. Henry W. Slocum, Jr., who was to become the second national singles champion, listed the Casino's advantages as well-kept courts, good accommodations for the players, and "the most beautiful women of the country" among the spectators. They were there as much to be seen as to see; courtside conversation was often brisker than the play, and many a point was lost because a player had his eye on a belle instead of the ball.

There were, of course, a few young men who concentrated on the new sport with all the fervor they were wont to devote to baseball or bicycling. Such a one was Richard D. Sears, of Harvard, who won the first official national championship at Newport in the summer of 1881 and continued to win every year thereafter until 1888, when he retired from competition because of a neck injury. A diligent student of the game, he kept up with every innovation of style and technique, contributing several himself. His record of seven consecutive U.S.L.T.A. singles championships has never been matched, although two other famous players compiled a *total* of seven wins each —William A. Larned, between 1901 and 1911, and William T. "Big Bill" Tilden, in the 1920's.

During Sears's reign in the 1880's tennis assumed its modern and presumably permanent form, having reached maturity in only one decade. The net was officially set at its present height, three feet at the center and three

feet six inches at the posts, in 1882. With the base lines thirty-nine feet from the net, a nice balance had now been achieved—a balance, it should be said, that makes tennis nearly unique among leading competitive sports.

In baseball the harder a man can clout the ball the better; and if he knocks it out of the stadium, he has a home run. In hockey a hard-slung puck is usually prevented from going out by the sides of the rink. In football, soccer, and basketball, a ball projected out of the playing area temporarily halts the game but does not change the score. In tennis, if you hit the ball out, your opponent gets a point. Yet the subtle balance between net height and length of the court means that you can hit the ball with all your strength and still see it fall inside the lines—if you have the skill to hit it correctly. A ball with an off-the-racket velocity of a hundred miles per hour, struck from one base line at a height of just over four feet and with an initially level trajectory, will skim the net and strike the ground about a half second later, well within the court on the other side. Few, even among the experts, have the power and control to make such a shot consistently. But the game has a beautiful self-adjusting character. The more gently the ball is hit, the more generously it can be allowed to soar above the net with plenty of margin for error and still no danger of its going out. Serious beginners are almost automatically accommodated, yet reckless incompetence is severely penalized.

As the years went by, the peculiar ballistics of tennis led the top players to startling new ploys. The first British champion, Spencer W. Gore, discovered that if he moved up close to the net, he could dispose of the ball as it came over and before it could hit the ground. In other words, he discovered the volley. This was regarded as ungenteel by some players, notably those whom Gore had beaten; but a close search of the rules turned up nothing against it. The countervailing weapon was soon introduced: the controlled pop-up, or lob, which sailed neatly over the volleyer's head to land near the base line. Then a fierce competitor named William Renshaw— another Englishman—learned to run back under a lob and hit it on the way down, like a serve, thus producing an ungettable shot known admiringly as a Renshaw smash. Renshaw fought a series of verbal and court duels with another ranking player, H. F. Lawford, who had developed an enormously powerful drive and who disdained the volley. For a while, that is. As a commentator observed in 1885, Lawford finally came over to the volley game himself, "finding that Mr. W. Renshaw invariably beat him."

The volley had come to stay, but its use among the better male players unfortunately widened the gender gap and turned mixed doubles into a game avoided by anyone who played tennis seriously. It was simply taken for granted that ladies had neither the wit, the strength, nor the agility to volley, and the instruction manuals of the 80's and 90's are full of admonitions to the effect that, as Dick Sears put it, "the volley game is not made for ladies." "With a few exceptions," declared a book on lawn tennis in 1885, "ladies never seem to know where the ball is going."

Part of the problem, as Sears gallantly recognized, was not innate inferiority but feminine styles of dress. Right to the end of the century, few ladies ventured out upon the court in anything but lawn-sweeping skirts, and hats were *de rigueur*. Sears hopefully recommended short skirts—that is, just above the ankle—and "a nice small hat" rather than "a great big hat that waggles about," but apparently it never occurred to him, or to anyone else, that such superficial adjustments could do much to offset what was assumed to be a natural deficiency. Ladies habitually served underhand until well after 1900, and anyone who broke that custom could expect to be regarded as a hussy.

Tennis dress for men started out on the casual side, and early pictures show a broad variety—knickers, tam-o'-shanters, long trousers of varied hues, colorful cravats, and bright blazers. Gradually, white became the favored color, and by the 90's fashionable players were seldom seen on the court in anything else. The regulation costume of long white trousers and a white shirt was to prevail for nearly a half century, giving way finally—in the 1930's—to the more practical shorts only after a considerable struggle between the innovators and the critics, who felt that the Lord clearly meant calves, knees, and thighs to remain covered on tennis courts. (Nobody has yet dared to appear in an important public match stripped to the waist, although the nature of the game would seem to make that as appropriate for tennis as it is for swimming or boxing.)

Despite the fact that the official name of the game has never changed from lawn tennis, good grass courts have always been scarce, and only a tiny percentage of players have ever played on one. Such a court is devilishly difficult to establish and maintain, and the advantages of less pleasant alternatives—clay, asphalt, and concrete—became obvious before the game was ten years old. In California, where the sport began to be highly popular around the turn of the century, concrete for some reason was the preferred material; elsewhere clay was the more usual substitute for grass. The last decade or so has seen increasing use of rubber or plastic composition.

The other appurtenances of the game—nets, balls, and rackets—evolved slowly during the early years of tennis, with relatively little change in the net, a bit more in the ball (which grew steadily more uniform and more lively), and the most of all in the racket. In this connection it probably is news to many players today that the

*The renowned Davis Cup stands before its donor, Dwight F. Davis, who in 1900 formed the first American Davis Cup team with two other Harvard men: Malcolm D. Whitman (on his right) and Holcombe Ward. They easily beat an English team.*

rules of the game have nothing whatever to say about the racket. It can be of any size, shape, or material, and the "standard" model is purely a convention. Nothing would prevent a player from entering a tennis tournament armed with a Ping-Pong racket or a baseball bat, if that suited his whim, although he might not do too well in the competition. In actuality, of course, the search has been for a well-balanced, more resilient racket that would impart more speed to the ball with less effort, and this has led to tighter and tighter stringing and—recently—to metal frames. Catgut (made, paradoxically, from sheepgut) is still preferred by most good players to the more durable nylon, which first made its appearance in tennis rackets shortly after World War II.

Everything considered, tennis changed far more in the first twenty-six years of its existence in America than it has in the seventy-one years since 1900. As the new century began, the game was being played much the way it is today, and it is altogether likely that the male champions of 1900 would give a good account of themselves were they to appear in a modern tournament. It was in that year, by the way, that regular international competition was launched in the name of what is now called the Davis Cup. Dwight F. Davis, of St. Louis, a well-fixed Harvard senior in 1900 and (with his classmate Holcombe Ward) a United States doubles champion, donated the now-famous silver bowl to the U.S.L.T.A. It was officially known as the International Lawn Tennis Challenge Trophy, and it was to go to whichever nation successfully challenged the current holder in a series of matches. Davis, Ward, and Malcolm D. Whitman, also a Harvard man, were the first American Davis Cup defenders, and they easily beat Great Britain, which made the mistake of sending over something less than its top-ranking players. (The British won the cup in 1903, however, and it was ten years before America won it back. Australasia had become a tennis power in the meantime, holding the cup from 1907 through 1911.) Dwight Davis later was prominent in government circles, serving as Secretary of War under Calvin Coolidge and as governor general of the Philippines from 1929 to 1932. He went right on playing tennis.

One thing that did change after 1900 was ladies' tennis, but this was more a part of the women's liberation movement, early phase, than it was a development of the game itself. In 1904 there appeared from California a fourteen-year-old girl named May Sutton, who proceeded to win every women's tournament in sight. Her tactics were not very ladylike, but they were highly effective: she ran hard for every ball that was out of easy reach; she served overhand; she volleyed whenever she got the chance; and she put every one of her approximately hundred and ten pounds behind every drive. May went on in 1905 to win the ladies' singles at Wimbledon—the first American of either sex to take the British championship. It was the beginning of the end of patball, underhand-serve tennis for women. Henceforth the aim would be to play as nearly like a man as possible—although another generation would go by before women shed enough layers of clothing to put them on an equal-opportunity basis with their male counterparts. The fact that in 1971 any man rated among the top ten in the

## TEN KINGS OF THE COURT

*Here are ten of the U.S. men's singles champions, spanning nearly ninety years of tennis history: (1) Richard D. Sears, first winner and a repeater for seven years (1881–87); (2) William A. Larned, also a seven-time champ (1901–2, 1907–11); (3) Maurice E. McLoughlin (1912–13); (4) William Johnston (1915, 1919); (5) William T. Tilden II, a third seven-time winner (1920–25, 1929); (6) H. Ellsworth Vines, Jr. (1931–32); (7) J. Donald Budge (1937–38); (8) John A. Kramer (1946–47); (9) Richard A. "Pancho" Gonzales (1948–49); (10) Arthur Ashe (1968). Gonzales, a kind of historical monument in himself, is still competing in big-time tennis twenty-two years after winning the championship.*

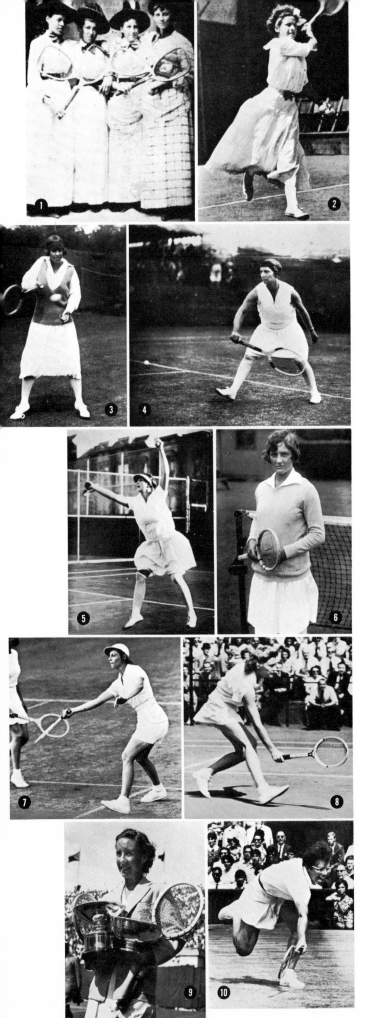

country could probably beat the first-ranked woman player, however, is something for women's lib to explain if it can.

Notwithstanding what evidently is a built-in difference of ability between the sexes, it is doubtful that tennis has any close rival as a first-rate spectator sport that is also superbly suited to the strictly amateur weekend player. The game is a bouncy reproach to the millions of sedentary sports fans who get a little fatter every week as they watch professional athletes perform on the baseball diamond or the gridiron. It has been estimated that four out of five spectators at the national championship matches at Forest Hills are tennis players themselves. It only takes two or four to play, and nowadays there are courts everywhere. The game is strenuous—increasingly so as one's skill improves—but if you keep at it, you can play safely, with great benefit to your health, from eight to eighty. Golf palls beside it, as far as exercise goes, and swimming ordinarily lacks the competitive element. Skiing is more difficult, more dangerous, and more expensive.

Tennis is also an exceedingly satisfying game psychologically and emotionally. By tradition it is polite—a courtly game. You do not haze your opponent or try to hit him with the ball, and you give him the benefit of the doubt on close calls. At the same time you may work off a great deal of aggression by swatting the ball as viciously as you can—and in one match of just ordinary duration, a tennis player hits the ball more times than a professional baseball player is likely to from May to September. Dramatic reversals are common, and there is no such thing as being hopelessly behind in tennis. Many a player has saved himself at match point by a cool or desperate maneuver and then gone on to win game, set, and ultimately match.

All in all, tennis is the great international game, and it shows every sign of attracting more followers each year. Despite some disconcerting innovations, such as the synthetic "turf" that has displaced real grass at a number of eminent clubs, it has been essentially the same game for nearly a century, and Major Wingfield and Miss Mary Outerbridge would seem to deserve a modern salute: Right on!

## AND ELEVEN QUEENS

*Our first picture, upper left, shows two U.S. women's singles champions: Ellen F. Hansell, the first winner in 1887 (right, checkered dress), and Bertha L. Townsend (1888–89) on the left; (2) May G. Sutton (1904); (3) Molla Bjurstedt Mallory (1915–18, 1920–22, 1926—an eight-time winner); (4) Hazel V. Hotchkiss (1909–11 and in 1919 as Mrs. Hazel Hotchkiss Wightman—later the donor of the Wightman Cup for women's international competition); (5) Helen N. Wills (1923–25, 1927–29, and in 1931 as Mrs. Helen Wills Moody); (6) Helen Jacobs (1932–35); (7) Alice Marble (1936, 1938–40); (8) Pauline M. Betz (1942–44, 1946); (9) Maureen Connolly (1951–53); (10) Billie Jean King (1967).*

*Framed in a classic Dutch landscape, C-47 transports tow glider-borne infantry to the support of the First Allied Airborne Army in Operation Market-Garden. These reinforcements were slated for U.S. 82nd Airborne Division paratroopers who landed at Nijmegen.*

# Hell's Highway to Arnhem

It would have taken considerable effort to locate an Allied fighting man on the battle line in Western Europe on September 10, 1944, who doubted that the end of the war was just around the corner. To American GI's and British Tommies up front, heartened by six weeks of unrelieved victory, the chances of being home by Christmas were beginning to look very good indeed.

Those six weeks had been spectacular. Since late July, when the Anglo-American armies had burst out of their Normandy beachhead, the vaunted German army had fled for its life. Narrowly escaping encirclement at Falaise, nearly trapped against the Seine, harried out of Paris, driven pell-mell toward the Siegfried Line, which guarded the borders of the Third Reich itself, the German forces in France had lost a half million men and 2,200 tanks and self-propelled guns. It was a rout, a blitzkrieg in reverse.

The optimism buoying the combat troops was not entirely shared by the Allied High Command, however. Supplies were critically short, and the enemy showed signs of getting himself sorted out. A hot inter-Allied argument—soon to be christened the Great Argument—was raging over the next strategic step. On September 10 the debate hit one of its peaks. The setting was the Brussels airport, the scene the personal aircraft of the Supreme Commander, Dwight D. Eisenhower. The principal debater was British Field Marshal Bernard Law Montgomery.

The meeting went badly from the start. Eisenhower, who had recently wrenched his knee in a forced landing during an inspection flight to the front, was confined to his plane. On arriving, Montgomery arrogantly demanded that Ike's administrative aide leave while his own stayed. Ever the patient conciliator, Eisenhower agreed. Montgomery then delivered himself of an increasingly violent attack on the Supreme Commander's conduct of the war. Rather than continuing the advance on Germany on a broad front, Montgomery argued for a halt to all offensive operations except for "one really powerful and full-blooded thrust" in his own sector, aimed toward the great German industrial complex in the Ruhr Valley and beyond.

"He vehemently declared," Eisenhower was later to write, "that . . . if we would support his 21st Army

*By* STEPHEN W. SEARS

*Dramatis personae of the battle for Arnhem. At upper left, Major General James M. Gavin of the U.S. 82nd Airborne loads his gear for the drop on Holland. The U.S. 101st Airborne's Major General Maxwell D. Taylor poses in the door of a C-47 at upper right. At right center, Field Marshal Walther Model, the German commander in the Arnhem sector, talks with an aide. Market-Garden was the brain child of Field Marshal Bernard L. Montgomery, talking (above) to war correspondents in 1944.*

Group with all supply facilities available he would rush right on to Berlin and, he said, end the war."

Eisenhower's temper rose with Montgomery's intemperance. Finally he leaned forward, put his hand on the Field Marshal's knee, and said: "Steady, Monty! You can't speak to me like that. I'm your boss!" Montgomery, who calculated his outbursts for effect, saw that he had gone too far and contritely apologized. Their discussion continued calmly enough, but their strategic differences remained.

When he left the meeting, however, Montgomery carried with him Eisenhower's approval of a plan codenamed Operation Market-Garden. If he had gained less than he sought, Montgomery at least had in Market-Garden what British war correspondent Chester Wilmot has described as "the last, slender chance of ending the German war in 1944."

In those early days of September the Allies had simply outrun their supply network. Armored units were stalled without gasoline. Replacements, food, ammunition, and spare parts were far below even minimum needs. Yet only by applying hard, continuous pressure on the enemy could the Allies hope to breach the Siegfried Line and win a bridgehead across the Rhine before winter— and perhaps even force a complete Nazi collapse.

Supply problems could not be solved overnight. The Allies had reached the German border 233 days ahead of their preinvasion timetable, and it would take weeks for logistics to catch up. In Eisenhower's view, just trying to reach the Rhine on the present supply shoestring was gamble enough. To approve Montgomery's "full-blooded thrust" without a solid logistic base and without the capability of making diversionary attacks elsewhere on the front was to invite its destruction. Better to advance to the Rhine on a broad front, Ike believed, and then pause to regroup and resupply before plunging on into the Third Reich at full strength.

Ike conceded that the strategic opportunities in Montgomery's northern sector were attractive—the vital Nazi arsenal of the Ruhr, the good "tank country" of the north German plain—and had granted supply priority to the 21st Army Group. Yet he was unwilling to rein in completely U.S. Lieutenant General Omar Bradley's 12th Army Group to the south, whose advance was aimed at the industrialized Saar region.

The Supreme Commander also carried a burden of quite a different sort: mediating between two eccentrics of towering military reputation. On the one hand, spearheading Bradley's army group, there was the flamboyant George Patton, a familiar sight in newsreels and on front pages throughout the Allied world. His Third Army tankers had covered the most ground and grabbed the most headlines in the race across France, and to the American public they seemed unstoppable.

Then there was Bernard Montgomery, victor of El Alamein and Britain's great hero, with an acrid manner and an insufferable ego that invariably grated on his American colleagues. To halt either Patton or Montgomery at the other's expense might open a serious fissure in the Anglo-American coalition. Dwight Eisenhower was too good a student of coalition warfare to allow that to happen.

In any case the issues that September were clear: how to keep the pursuit from bogging down; how to break the barrier of the Siegfried Line; how to gain a bridgehead across the Rhine. Operation Market-Garden offered to resolve all three.

By September 10 the staging area for Market-Garden was secure. At dusk that day elements of Montgomery's 21st Army Group crossed the Meuse-Escaut Canal in Belgium, close to the Dutch border. Most of Belgium was in Allied hands, including Antwerp, the great port so badly needed for logistic support of Eisenhower's armies. Antwerp was useless, however, until German troops were routed from the banks of the Scheldt estuary that linked the port with the North Sea.

Operation Market-Garden, scheduled for September 17, involved a sudden, one hundred-mile thrust from the Meuse-Escaut Canal almost due north into Holland, crossing the Lower Rhine at the city of Arnhem and reaching all the way to the Zuider Zee. If successful, it would completely outflank the Siegfried Line and win a coveted Rhine bridgehead. In addition, it would cut Holland in two, trapping thousands of German troops and isolating the chief launching sites of the deadly v-2 ballistic missiles that were pummelling London.

With these objectives in hand Montgomery was confident that Eisenhower would have no choice but to fully support his plan to seize the Ruhr and drive on toward Berlin. Thus, the Field Marshal declared, the war could be won "reasonably quickly."

Eisenhower was less sanguine. He cautioned Montgomery that the opening of Antwerp could not long be delayed. Much would depend on Market-Garden succeeding quickly and at minimum cost.

As bold as the plan itself was the technique designed to carry it out. The Dutch countryside was ideally suited to defense, marshy and heavily wooded and cut by numerous waterways: in the span of sixty-five miles the single highway running north from the Belgian border to Arnhem crossed no less than three canals, two small rivers, and three major streams—the Maas, the Waal, and the Lower Rhine. Montgomery proposed to lay a "red carpet" for his ground forces over this difficult terrain by using Eisenhower's entire strategic reserve, the paratroops of the First Allied Airborne Army. Their mission was to seize the bridges over these eight waterways in a massive surprise invasion from the sky. This airdrop

CONTINUED ON PAGE 94

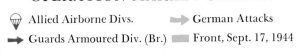

## OPERATION MARKET-GARDEN

Allied Airborne Divs.          German Attacks

Guards Armoured Div. (Br.)     Front, Sept. 17, 1944

*The constricted front on which Operation Market-Garden operated is evident on this map. The parachute symbols designate the initial airdrop zones of the 101st Division (between Eindhoven and Uden), the 82nd Division (between Grave and Nijmegen), and the 1st British Airborne (at Arnhem). The Allied ground forces were spearheaded by the Guards Armoured Division of the British Second Army. Walther Model's two Panzer divisions anchored the crucial German defenses at the Nijmegen and Arnhem bridges.*

# A CANAL,

# A MAN, A PLAN,

# PANAMA!

*The Canal's great scope spurred artists to heroic scenes of the machines, left, and men, above—T.R., Stevens, Goethals, and Gorgas—who conquered the Isthmus. Likewise inspired, we have titled this story with a verbal rarity, a famous palindrome.*

THE BIG DITCH HAD SO FAR BEEN A COLOSSAL FLOP, AND TEDDY

ROOSEVELT DESPERATELY NEEDED AN ENGINEERING GENIUS WHO

COULD TAKE OVER THE JOB AND "MAKE THE DIRT FLY." THE

ANSWER WAS NOT THE FAMOUS GOETHALS, BUT A MAN WHOM

HISTORY HAS FORGOTTEN

*By* DAVID G. McCULLOUGH

The Panama Canal was the biggest, most costly thing Americans had ever attempted beyond their borders, as was plain to everyone in the summer of 1905, and particularly to the man most responsible for the project, Theodore Roosevelt. But as Roosevelt also knew full well by then, and as the American people were beginning to suspect, the Canal was so far a colossal flop. Earlier, when a group of Yale professors had challenged the legality of the American presence in Panama, Roosevelt had answered grandly, "Tell them I am going to make the dirt

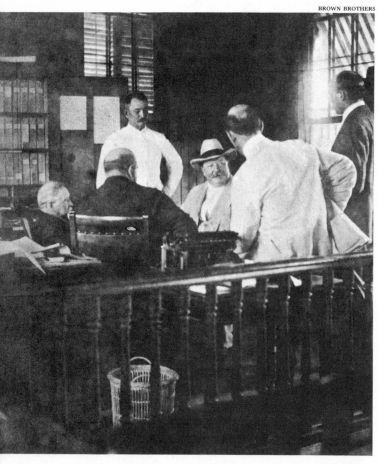

*In a rare, informal 1905 photo, Stevens stands on the right of portly Secretary of War Taft—sightseeing heavy brass in every sense.*

fly on the Isthmus." That was supposed to have squashed all such talk and fixed public attention on ends instead of means. Henceforth the President would speak of building the Canal as though it were a mighty battle in which the national honor was at stake. It was just the way the ill-fated Frenchman, Ferdinand de Lesseps, had talked twenty years earlier.

In Washington, however, Roosevelt's seven-man Canal Commission seemed incapable of agreeing on anything, let alone how to direct history's most massive engineering

effort from a distance of two thousand miles. In Panama things were in a fearful muddle. There were no plans to go by, no proper equipment to work with. Nobody had any real say, and nobody seemed to give a damn about building a canal. Among some of the engineers there the situation was looked upon as a disgrace to the profession, and among influential Republicans back home it was viewed as a potential disaster of alarming proportions.

Ships arriving in New York were bringing home more men than they were taking down—hundreds that spring. The newspapers were filled with grim, discouraging accounts by young Americans back from "that sink hole." Every white man in Panama was afflicted with running sores, it was said. Workers were sleeping six to a room and eating high-priced food that would sicken a dog. The place was crawling with vermin, and there was absolutely nothing to do—no music, no churches, no sports, no books. The boredom alone, according to one eyewitness, was "appalling."

But worst by far were the stories of yellow fever and malaria. There had been an outbreak of yellow fever in April; now, supposedly, an epidemic was raging. The "dead train" to Mount Hope Cemetery was making daily trips. Accounts of health conditions were, it happens, largely distorted. There was, in truth, still comparatively little yellow fever considering the number of men on the Isthmus—134 cases and thirty-four deaths during the eighteen months of the so-called epidemic. But the impression was that the Americans were fast going the way of the French, who had lost thousands of lives trying to do the same thing in the same tropical wilderness.

When de Lesseps began his Panama venture, the finest civil engineers in France had enlisted in the work, believing it to be a noble cause for the glory of France. Now it was exceedingly difficult to get any young American to sign up.

And then suddenly, with no warning at all, the chief engineer of the Canal, a Chicago railroad man named John F. Wallace, resigned his job. He was getting twenty-five thousand dollars a year for his services in Panama, but he said he had had a better offer and gave no further explanation. Roosevelt was furious. And when Wallace came up to New York from Panama to meet with Secretary of War William Howard Taft, who had overall responsibility for the Canal, there was a stormy session in Taft's room at the Manhattan Hotel. Taft ripped into Wallace for deserting his duty for "mere lucre." Stunned by Taft's outburst, Wallace asked for time to talk things over, but Taft told him his resignation would be accepted immediately.

The news that Wallace had quit set off something very near panic in Panama, where nobody thought that his motive was monetary. Wallace lived in mortal terror of yellow fever, the story went. Incredible as it may seem,

66

when he and his wife first arrived on the Isthmus, they had among their belongings two expensive coffins.

The meeting between Taft and Wallace took place on June 22, 1905, and the newspapers made much of it. A few days later the job of chief engineer was quietly offered to another railroad man from Chicago. Roosevelt had decided to put the Canal in the hands of somebody he had never met and knew little about—except for what the railroad magnate James J. Hill, a Democrat and no special admirer of Roosevelt, had to say for him.

His name was John Frank Stevens, and he had been described by Hill, in a conversation with Taft, as the best civil engineer in America. Hill had good reason to know. Stevens had played an outstanding role in the building of the Hill-owned Great Northern Railway Company. Stevens turned the offer down at first, but then he was called upon by an unofficial emissary—William Nelson Cromwell, New York corporation lawyer, lobbyist for the Panamanians, Republican mystery man, and behind-the-scenes arranger of shadowy deals. Cromwell told Stevens that a failure to build the Canal would be disastrous for the administration, and after an hour or more of what Stevens later described as "silver-tongued arguments" from Cromwell, Stevens consented, with conditions. (One of Stevens' sons later said his mother also urged Stevens to say Yes, telling him that his whole career had been in preparation for this great engineering command.)

On July 14, at Oyster Bay, Roosevelt and Stevens shook hands for the first time. The day, appropriately enough, was terribly hot and humid. Stevens had been invited to lunch, along with Theodore P. Shonts (still another railroad man, but a business executive rather than an engineer), whom Roosevelt had named chairman of his brand-new, streamlined Canal Commission.

According to Stevens' recollection, Roosevelt admitted outright that things were in a "devil of a mess" at Panama. Stevens told Roosevelt that he was taking the job against his real wishes; that he was a man of few words, and those could be blunt on occasion. His conditions were these: he wanted a free hand, no trouble from bureaucrats or politicians, and an understanding that he would stay with the work until he was sure of its success or he had proved it a failure. Roosevelt, Stevens said later, agreed immediately and told Stevens to skip channels and report directly to him.

In another week or so Stevens was on his way to the Canal Zone, that "graveyard of reputations," as Secretary of State Root called it. In the next year and a half Stevens would accomplish far more than his superiors in Washington could possibly have expected of him. The choice of Stevens was, as a matter of fact, among the wisest moves Theodore Roosevelt ever made, as Roosevelt himself said at the time. More than any other single man,

except for Roosevelt, Stevens was to make the decisions that would bring the Panama Canal to completion.

In the Roosevelt Memorial Hall at the American Museum of Natural History there is a mural by William Andrew Mackay, which gives Stevens his rightful place of importance in the story of the Canal. It is, in this respect, a rarity. On the left, in the background, behind two canal workers, stands George Washington Goethals, the very able Army engineer who would replace Stevens. On the right, behind two more canal workers, is William

*It was Roosevelt's turn to visit in 1906. Gleefully, the President sat in a steam shovel to try his hand at making the dirt fly.*

C. Gorgas, the Army doctor in charge of sanitation at Panama and the one principal in the building of the Canal who was on the Isthmus from start to finish. In the center, presented full figure, side by side, are Roosevelt, holding a sheet of plans, and Stevens, who appears to be explaining to Roosevelt how the Canal will be built.

When the Canal was finished, Goethals would call it Stevens' monument. The world could not give Stevens too much credit, Goethals would write. But in the time since, the world has given Stevens scarcely any credit at all. He has been strangely overlooked by history. His name now means little to any but a handful of civil engineers, some scholars of western exploration, a few elderly railroad men, and two or three Canal historians. The average student of American history has never heard of Stevens. Today the only engineer popularly identified with the Canal is the Army man, Goethals. That this is so, however, seems due largely to the particular make-up of John F. Stevens as well as that of the man who put him in charge at the Canal—Theodore Roosevelt. The the time the Canal job came along he was a vice president of the Rock Island Railroad in Chicago. During his years in the West, and particularly those with Hill, Stevens had educated himself as thoroughly as any man in the profession. He had earned a reputation as a worker and about the ablest engineer in the business. Moreover, he had been treed by wolves, chased by Indians, struck down by Mexican fevers, marooned by blizzards, given up for lost on more than one occasion; had developed a robust physique that seemed impervious to climate; and

*Digging the Canal meant war on disease and boredom as well as on natural obstacles. It required the provision of simple but sanitary housing, far left, and mess halls, left center, where hard-working personnel could fill up on robust American meals for thirty-five cents.*

impulsive T.R. was at once taken with Stevens, who described himself later as "a kind of politic 'roughneck,' who did not possess too deep a veneration for the vagaries of constituted authority." This was just what the situation in Panama demanded. But later, when Stevens left the job, Roosevelt—just as impulsively, it would appear—denied him his true place in the Canal's history.

Stevens was fifty-two in 1905, powerfully built and strikingly handsome, with a somewhat swarthy complexion and a thick black mustache. He had been raised on a farm near West Gardiner, Maine. Like many other engineers of his time he never received any formal training, although virtually all his career would be spent building railroads. He first did some surveying in Maine and then went west in 1873. He worked as a rodman in Minneapolis, a section hand in Texas—driving spikes at a dollar ten cents a day—and eventually as an assistant engineer laying out lines for a half dozen western railroads, including the Canadian Pacific. In 1876 he married Harriet O'Brien of Dallas, Texas. They had five children, two of whom died in infancy.

In 1889 Stevens went to work for James J. Hill, the celebrated "Empire Builder" of the Northwest, and by had become something of a legend in Montana, where, in the dead of winter in 1889, he had found the "lost" Marias Pass through the Rockies.

Stevens' discovery of the pass saved Hill more than a hundred miles and gave the Great Northern the lowest grade of any railroad over the divide. Later, in the Cascades, Stevens found another important pass that, against his wishes, was named for him. By the time he moved on in 1903, Stevens had built bridges, tunnels, and more than a thousand miles of track for Hill (quite probably as much track as any man in the world), and the Great Northern was recognized as the best-engineered railroad in the country.

Stevens later called Hill the finest man he ever knew. And once he got to Panama, at the end of July, 1905, Stevens quickly demonstrated a number of Hill's more noted qualities. Like Hill, he believed in giving subordinates as much authority as possible and then holding them responsible for results. He was decisive, intelligent, highly intolerant of incompetence, and never did he leave anyone in doubt as to who was boss. But it was his ability to instill spirit and personal loyalty among workingmen that gave Stevens his most obvious resemblance to Hill and had the most immediate effect at Panama.

Stevens found the situation a good deal worse than it had been described to him. At high tide tons of garbage drifted about the piers at Colon, the terminal where ships from New York docked. Wharves were crowded with goods nobody seemed able to account for and men with little to do. Colon itself and Panama City, the opposite terminal, were vile, depressing places with foul drinking water, dreadful food, and streets strewn with filth. The American workers all seemed possessed by fear of yellow

announce that the United States was pulling out and abandoning the whole project.

Since the Americans had taken over, surprisingly little had been done. Equipment left behind by the French, which Wallace had tried futilely to make do with, was nearly all too antiquated to be of value, and scarcely any new equipment was on hand. (Wallace had wanted to experiment at length with various kinds of steam shovels, dump cars, and other machinery before deciding on what to order.) The famous Panama Railroad had only one

*There were heartbreaking roadblocks like Cucaracha slide, right center, which dumped loose earth relentlessly into the Cut. But the polyglot work gangs, among them Panamanians, West Indians, Basques, and Italians (like those at far right), finally conquered them.*

fever. (Black laborers and others native to the Caribbean or Panama were largely immune.) And though the trouble to date was nearly all in their minds, there was still no guarantee that a real epidemic might not break out any day.

Few workers appeared to know what they were doing. For those who did there was a maddening tangle of red tape to cope with. At one point Stevens saw two new recruits from Martinique hoist a wheelbarrow full of dirt up onto the head of a third man, who carried it off that way. Carpenters were forbidden to saw boards over ten feet long without a signed permit. When he went out to Culebra Cut (later renamed Gaillard Cut), the place midway across the zone where the Canal would have to slice some nine miles through the mountain spine of the Isthmus, every steam shovel in sight was idle. "Nobody was working but the ants and the typists," he said.

There was, as he wrote, "no organization worthy of the name, no answerable head who could delegate authority and exact responsibility; no cooperation . . . between what might charitably be called departments . . ." When a first meeting with department heads was called shortly after Stevens' arrival, the men thought it was to

track, and its undersized rolling stock was twenty years out of date. There were no sidings and no warehouses. When somebody told Stevens there had been few collisions, he answered, "A collision has its good points as well as bad ones—it indicates that there is something moving on the railroad."

The Canal was to follow the line of the railroad, which was approximately the route the French had figured on. The French, contrary to popular opinion in the United States, had accomplished quite a lot considering the equipment they had. Their determination in the face of continual setbacks and death had been heroic to say the least, and almost certainly they would have succeeded had it not been for yellow fever and de Lesseps' insistence on a sea-level canal like the Suez. But the jungle had long since returned over most of the French work, and the forty-two-mile stretch between Colon and Panama City looked about as it had to Vasco Nuñez de Balboa, who had discovered the Isthmus four centuries earlier. There was still no final plan authorized by Washington, and Stevens had seventeen thousand men waiting to be told what to do.

Stevens' own plan was very simple. He would *prepare*

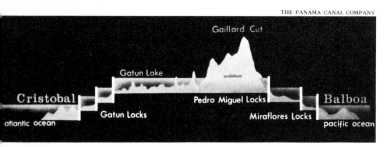

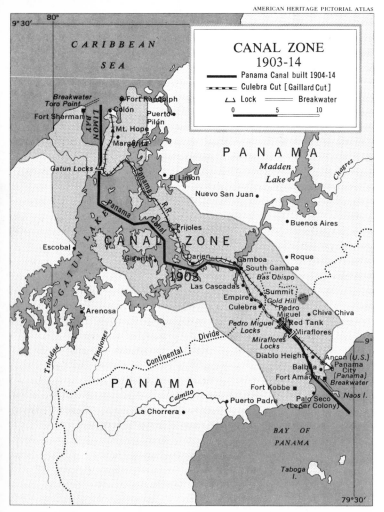

*The cross-sectional diagram of the lock system and the map below it illustrate some oddities of Canal travel. Vessels must "climb" up and down from sea level to get from ocean to ocean, in part via a lake. And, in seeming defiance of geography, the Pacific is reached from the Caribbean by sailing southeast.*

to dig a canal. Making dirt fly, he saw from the start, was not at all what was called for. That, he estimated, would be the easiest part of the job and it could wait. So he stopped all excavation and announced that it would not resume until he had everything ready (a very unpopular move back home where the American people were eager for news of progress).

His first step was to do something about morale, and that came easy to him. By nature he was not an "office engineer." He put on a pair of overalls and rubber boots and rapidly became a familiar sight up and down the line, riding the railroad, tramping through the jungle (he would walk the entire length of the Zone, surveying the scene and studying what the French had done), or out among the men talking to them in a way they had not been talked to before. "There are three diseases on the Isthmus," he told them, "yellow fever, malaria, and cold feet. And the worst of these is cold feet."

Any men who were not needed, now that the digging had stopped, he sent home. They would be hearing from him later, he said. The rest he put to work building decent housing, mess halls, hospitals, schoolhouses, churches, jails—whole communities. Under his direction approximately five thousand new buildings were built, old French facilities refurbished, streets paved, and new harbor installations, a sewage disposal plant, and water mains put in. He installed a telephone system. He established a commissary to feed the entire force at cost. He introduced refrigeration equipment, something unknown in Panama, and the men began eating dressed meats, eggs, and perishable vegetables for the first time. He built clubhouses and organized band concerts and a baseball league, with each settlement along the line getting up its own team. When a young clerk told him there were no funds available to build seven or eight home fields, Stevens said to charge them to sanitary expenses. For months he had twelve thousand men doing nothing but putting up buildings. The most imposing structure, the Tivoli Hotel, was rushed to completion when it became known that Roosevelt was coming down to visit.

Previous plans were for the chief engineer to be quartered in a palatial residence to be built overlooking Panama Bay. But Stevens wanted no part of that. He and his family would live on the side of Culebra Cut, he said, where he could watch the work progress from his front porch. So he had a plain house with a corrugated roof put up there.

But for all his talk of cold feet, Stevens had a very realistic fear of yellow fever and considered it the one overriding threat to success. He said as much only in private, but unlike his predecessor—or his successor—as chief engineer he had total confidence in the courtly and dedicated Gorgas, and he decided at the outset that giving Gorgas whatever he needed to do the job was the only sensible course.

Gorgas was the doctor who had rid Havana of yellow fever, but many people, completely discounting his mosquito theory, considered him a crank all the same. Commission Chairman Shonts, for example, wanted Stevens to fire Gorgas first thing. Stevens, however, with Roosevelt's blessing, made Gorgas the second most powerful man on the Isthmus and backed him up whenever his methods came under fire. Every dwelling in the Zone would be fumigated. Stagnant pools would be sprayed with kerosene, drainage ditches built, rain bar-

*The gigantic gates of the Pacific-side Miraflores locks would have graced any home in Swift's overgrown land of Brobdingnag.*

*Like a spunky sardine trying an aquarium designed for whales, the tug* Gatun *makes a test trip through Gatun locks in 1913.*

*The Gatun locks admitted through traffic in August, 1914. A milestone in progress was gained even as World War I began.*

rels dumped, grass kept cut—everything possible to destroy the breeding places of the stegomyia and anopheles mosquitoes, the respective carriers of yellow fever and malaria. And all new buildings were fitted out with wire screens. Gorgas' original budget for medical supplies had been fifty thousand dollars; before he was through, Stevens would sign requisitions for ninety thousand dollars for window screening alone.

By October there would be only a few cases of yellow fever; by December, just one. After that there would be none at all, and the Zone would remain "as safe as a health resort," as Roosevelt put it. Indeed, no labor force in history had ever been so handsomely provided for.

Stevens saw the job of building the Canal itself as chiefly one of transporting dirt rather than digging it. Culebra Cut was, in his eyes, a gigantic railroad cut—nothing more. All that was needed was a proper system to haul the dirt out. He was to write:

To get the maximum efficiency out of any loading machine, steam shovel or dragline, the boom must be kept swinging every possible minute of the time. And this can only be accomplished by keeping empty cars, or trucks, always at hand to receive their loads from the machines. In this case it was wholly a matter of steam railroad operation.

This, of course, was precisely what he knew best.

The little Panama Railroad was overhauled and double-tracked with heavier rails. Most important of all, he devised an elaborate but elastic system of tracks leading out of Culebra Cut, whereby loaded cars always ran on a downgrade. The Cut itself he would slice back with gigantic steam shovels operating along a series of long steps, or benches, as they are known in surface mining, a subject with which Stevens had had some experience in the iron-ore fields of Minnesota. The material to be excavated was a miserable combination of clay and shale that, once exposed, had almost no stability. During the rainy season, or more than half the year, sudden cloudbursts would bring on terrible slides along the Cut. The French, during their stay on the Isthmus, had found it everything they could do just to keep pace with the slides.

The simplest way to cope with the problem—the only way, really—was to keep digging at the sides of the Cut, reducing the angle all the time. Since there was ample room in which to work, no pre-existing structures in the way, or other traffic of any kind, the Cut, in theory at least, could be as broad as was necessary. So the main objective was to marshal the right equipment in sufficient quantity. It was all a matter of "magnitude not miracles," Stevens wrote.

Stevens knew exactly what was needed in the way of machinery and wasted no time experimenting. By the time he was ready to begin digging, he had assembled a construction "plant" such as had never been seen before

CONTINUED ON PAGE 100

71

# To·The·Flag

It has been said that true patriotism never flags; Dr. Samuel Johnson went further, declaring that "patriotism is the last refuge of a scoundrel." Certainly, in the panorama of American history, many a rogue can be detected peering from behind the American flag, and today a red, white, and blue decal is no guarantee of anything.

One might have corresponding doubts about the Pledge of Allegiance, which, after all, is a type of loyalty oath—and everyone knows that any traitor worth the name will unblushingly swear to anything, while he has riot and sedition in his heart. Actions do speak louder than words.

Nevertheless, the Pledge of Allegiance has been taken very seriously in this nation, and court battles continue over whether children should or should not be required to recite it as part of a school exercise. In view of this it is a somewhat surprising fact that its history is so short and erratic. The pledge was not written until 1892 and did not receive congressional blessing until fifty years afterward; it has been rephrased three times; and it has been the focus of controversy throughout its career.

The Founding Fathers never dreamed of asking citizens to swear their allegiance; the only oath prescribed in the Constitution is the simple one taken by a President at his inauguration. When the Pledge of Allegiance was conceived, it was part of a promotion campaign undertaken by *The Youth's Companion*, a weekly magazine that featured uplifting, moralistic adventure stories for children.

In 1888 *The Youth's Companion* embarked on a program of "advancing patriotism" by encouraging the flying of The Stars and Stripes "over every schoolhouse." The campaign was notable in view of the void left by the nation's lawmakers; there was no federal law stipulating where, when, or how the American flag should be displayed, and worse—in the eyes of many Americans—no restriction whatsoever on its use in advertisements and trademarks or on a wide variety of products. Lemon wrappers, doormats, tents, and underwear were adorned with Old Glory, and distillers proudly emblazoned their names on the flag for display outside liquor shops.

A grand opportunity presented itself as the four-hundredth anniversary of Christopher Columbus' voyage

*For many years, when the pledge was recited, the flag was saluted in a variety of ways. These Washington, D.C., schoolchildren,*

# Invented as part of a magazine promotional scheme in 1892, the Pledge of Allegiance has had a controversial career right from the start

*By* NAT BRANDT

*photographed in 1899 by Frances Benjamin Johnston, are giving a version similar to the palm-over-heart salute that is now standard.*

to the New World approached in 1892. *The Youth's Companion* seized the initiative and persuaded a national convention of state educators to set up a National Public School Celebration to mark the event. Details for the special school exercises were worked out by a committee that met in the magazine's offices in Boston, with Francis M. Bellamy, an ordained Baptist minister who was one of the editors, serving as chairman. A twenty-three-word affirmation of loyalty written at the magazine—and proudly entitled "The Youth's Companion Flag Pledge" —was made an integral part of the school celebrations.

The ceremonies were timed to coincide with the dedication of the Columbian Exposition in Chicago. On October 19, 1892, pupils in that city gathered in assembly halls to hear a special proclamation from President Benjamin Harrison. Then, as they stood at attention, a color guard brought in the flag; as it was unfurled, the children saluted, fingertips to forehead, and said:

*I pledge allegiance to my flag and to the Republic for which it stands: one nation, indivisible, with liberty and justice for all.*

*The Youth's Companion* afterward boasted that twelve million children recited its pledge in similar exercises that same week—which would have included just about every boy and girl in every school in the nation's forty-four states, even those who might have been sick or playing hooky. In many schools the military salute gave way to a number of variations. In some the children held the right arm across the chest, palm downward; in others they extended the right hand toward the flag in what would now be taken as a Nazi salute. Everywhere the words of the pledge underwent strange transformations when young patriots tried to memorize them: "I pledge a *legion*..." became an all-too-common slip, as did "to the Republic for *witches' tan*..." and "one nation, *invisible*..."

Nevertheless, the fervor of the phrases took such hold on the nation's mind that more and more schools each year made recitation of the pledge a first-thing-in-the-morning ritual. Legislators in New York State, which had already taken the initiative in legislation to prohibit desecration of the flag, voted in 1910 to order the pledge said each school day. Such acceptance was bound to lead to tributes to the author, whose name might have be-

73

come as familiar to schoolchildren as Francis Scott Key's. Unfortunately, two persons were singled out for credit, and few people today would remember either: Bellamy, who had chaired the Columbus celebration committee, and James B. Upham, a junior partner of the Perry Mason Company, publishers of *The Youth's Companion.*

Upham died in 1905 without ever claiming authorship. However, when Bellamy, who was then no longer on the staff, sought the honor a few years later, *The Youth's Companion* initiated the dead man's claim. Upham, it asserted in a pamphlet published in 1917, had written the pledge "in tentative form," which was then "moulded" into final form by members of the firm and editors. Bellamy, the magazine insisted, "was not the author . . ."

There, one would think, the matter should have ended, but no—Bellamy persisted and was so persuasive that when he died in 1931 the *New York Times,* in his obituary, unequivocally said he had written the pledge. Upham's descendants cried foul, and the families of both men started taking pot shots at each other's claims. The United States Flag Assocation tried to settle the controversy in 1939; it asked two historians and a political scientist to sift the evidence from the two factions. Their conclusion—that Bellamy was the author—was, however, challenged by a one-man, self-appointed committee named Gridley Adams. Adams, an expert on the flag whose maternal great-great-grandfather had roomed with Nathan Hale at Yale, said the data clearly indicated that Upham had dictated the words to Bellamy.

Adams deluged the *World Almanac* with letters until, in its 1950 edition, the yearly publication conceded that Bellamy had written the pledge "at the suggestion" of Upham. There the seesaw dispute rested until 1957, when, at the urging of Representative Kenneth B. Keating, whose district covered Bellamy's hometown of Rome, New York, a special research team of the Library of Congress pronounced Bellamy the author.

Meanwhile, the fate of the pledge had become linked with Adams' chief concern—the proper use and display of the flag. By 1920 more than twenty patriotic organizations had each published civilian flag codes of their own, no two of which were alike. Adams brooded continually about the way the flag was ignominiously hung over speakers' platforms and carelessly draped over statues at unveilings. After an intensive study of heraldry, he drew some sketches to describe how and when the flag should be flown. (His most fervent admonition was that the canton, where the stars are, should always be on the dexter, or right, side of the flag, the position of honor— that is, to the viewer's left.) Adams showed his sketches to a neighbor, cartoonist Clare Briggs, who reprinted them in his column in the New York *Herald Tribune* in 1922. The reader response was so overwhelming and so critical (most patriotic societies took issue with Adams'

---

## MORNING GREETINGS TO OLD GLORY

*A personal reminiscence by our regular contributor Francis Russell*

There I am in corduroy knickerbockers and black cotton stockings, standing beside my desk at attention in Miss Sykes's Third Grade room of the Martha A. Baker School in Mattapan. The time is the last month or so of the War that is going to End All Wars and Make the World Safe for Democracy. Our boys Over There—spearheaded by the Yankee Division—are punching holes in the Hindenburg Line. The Huns are running in terror; the Beast of Berlin and the Clown Prince are trembling in their shiny spurred boots. We are pledging allegiance. Most of us wear lozenge-shaped Junior Red Cross buttons, though I, in a subsequently regretted surge of affection, gave mine to Marion Henries. Miss Sykes, for all her patriotic fervor, insists on the decencies. Edwin McDonald is not allowed to wear his Celluloid pin that reads "To H–LL with Kaiser Bill."

Looking back over a half century to that Third Grade room with its mud-colored walls, relieved only by W. Strutt's framed sepia picture, *And a Little Child Shall Lead Them,* I find myself caught up in a triple memory of Miss Sykes—blowing the pitch for us on her harmonica; walking up and down with a minatory ruler, while our pens traced the curlicued inanities of the Palmer Method; above all, leading us in the Pledge of Allegiance.

The pledge was new to Boston that September, as was the silk flag that hung to the right of Miss Sykes's desk— symbols that the School Committee, in a burst of patriotism, had just adopted. Our day began with Miss Sykes's unconstitutional reading of the Bible. Then we stood at attention facing the flag, as did Miss Sykes. "I," she exclaimed loudly, and paused. We raised our right hands to our foreheads, fingers and thumbs extended stiffly, while our left hands were pressed with equal stiffness to our sides.

"I pledge allegiance to my flag . . ."

At the word "flag" our hands shot forward in what Mussolini would shortly define as the "Roman salute" and Hitler, somewhat belatedly, as the "German greeting."

". . . one nation, intervisible with liberty and justice, for all."

Woe to anyone who in that solemn moment was chewing gum! Miss Sykes pounced on him like a terrier on a rat. In the days when small boys still wore collar buttons, her shakings left a semipermanent indentation in the throat.

version) that the War Department, although limited only to issuing flag guides for the Army and the Navy, unofficially let it be known that it supported Adams.

The one-man crusade also attracted the attention of the National Americanism Commission of the American Legion, which called a national meeting of patriotic groups to work out a common flag code. The conference was held in Washington, D.C., in 1923. With the War Department's backing, Adams was chosen by the delegates as permanent chairman of a new National Flag Code Committee to settle, once and for all, how civilians should be advised to fly the flag.

Adams immediately proposed that the Pledge of Allegiance, as it was now being called, should be part of such a flag code. He also made two recommendations. He urged that the words "my flag" be dropped in favor of "the Flag of the United States." ("I didn't like a pledge that any Hottentot could subscribe to," he remarked in an unconscious and unwarranted tribute to the government of South Africa.) Adams also recommended that instead of saluting the flag when reciting the pledge, civilians should place their right hands over their hearts —men with hat in hand, if wearing one. Both proposals were unanimously adopted by the delegates.

When Adams returned the following year to a second national flag conference, he took the opportunity to clarify further the rephrasing already agreed upon. This time the words "of America" were added to the pledge so that it now began, "I pledge allegiance to the Flag of the United States of America . . ." ("I thought people ought to be sure which united states they're talking about," Adams explained, having evidently learned about Brazil and Mexico.)

His successes notwithstanding, Adams still hoped that the federal government would adopt his flag code, thus adding officialdom's blessing and the permanency of law. For years he pressed congressmen to introduce flag bills, but ran into apathy.

It took the emotional zeal of World War II to make Congress finally adopt an official flag code, the first set of such rules issued since the nation was founded. Public Law 623 was passed in June, 1942, and revised, after Adams made some salient suggestions, in Public Law 829, which was enacted that December. The pledge was adopted as part of the code. It now read, after some minor changes in punctuation and capitalization:

*I pledge allegiance to the flag of the United States of America and to the republic for which it stands, one nation, indivisible, with liberty and justice for all.*

Even before it was made official, the pledge became the focus of legal attacks by religious and conscientious objectors. In 1940 a Pennsylvania couple, who were members of the Jehovah's Witnesses, insisted that a school regulation requiring children to recite the pledge

*James B. Upham*

*Francis M. Bellamy*

and salute the flag each day was contrary to the Book of Exodus' injunction against servitude to any graven image. Their argument was ultimately rejected by the Supreme Court, which upheld a state's right to impose the pledge. Three years later, however, the Court reversed its previous decision in a suit brought by a West Virginia couple, declaring that no one could "force citizens to confess by word or act" their loyalty. Subsequent decisions broadened this ruling, and today no child or adult can be compelled to recite the pledge or even stand during the ceremony—a freedom that is not always honored in practice.

The words of the Pledge of Allegiance managed to remain unchanged for a little more than ten years; then, once again, a war—the Korean—served as an impetus to patriotism. In April, 1953, Representative Louis C. Rabaut of Michigan received a letter from a man who suggested adding two words to the pledge that its author, the Reverend Mr. Bellamy, apparently never thought of —"under God." Rabaut was impressed by the idea— Lincoln had used those very words in his Gettysburg Address—and he introduced a resolution in the House of Representatives to amend the pledge. The proposal drew a chorus of approval from most churches, labor unions, patriotic groups, radio stations, and newspapers. But there were dissenters, too; though fewer in number, they were just as vocal. The Unitarian Ministers Association and the Freethinkers of America charged that the addition would violate religious freedom as implicit in the First Amendment's guarantee of separation of church and state. Somebody suggested that everything would be all right if a further addition were made: the words "if any" after "under God." "Everyone," a citizen wrote to the *New York Times*, "has to believe in God if he wants to pledge allegiance to the flag. How is this consistent with the end of the Pledge of Allegiance, '. . . with liberty and justice for all'?"

CONTINUED ON PAGE 104

# THE UNTOLD DELIGHTS OF DULUTH

*A few dazzling words about that emerging metropolis, delivered in 1871 by
Congressman J. Proctor Knott. Edited for 1971 visitors by David G. McCullough*

On January 27, 1871, a forty-year-old congressman from Kentucky sought recognition on the floor of the United States House of Representatives. Upon being recognized by the Speaker, the Honorable James G. Blaine, the congressman expressed dissatisfaction with the amount of time he had been allotted on past occasions and so requested, and was granted, one full, uninterrupted half hour to speak his mind. The congressman was a Democrat, an able lawyer, ambitious, learned in the classics, and generally well liked by his colleagues. He also had a name that seemed designed especially for being chiselled in stone or signed with a flourish on documents of state. His name was J. Proctor Knott.

Still, despite all this, J. Proctor Knott was little known outside Kentucky's Fourth District or the cloakrooms on Capitol Hill. In the next half hour, however, addressing himself to an obscure bill then before the House, he would change that. He would take up the question of whether federal lands ought to be given to the St. Croix and Lake Superior Railroad in order to build a new line that would run from Hudson, Wisconsin, on the St. Croix River to Superior, Wisconsin, located at the western end of Lake Superior and, as it happened, close by a scraggly Minnesota village of some three thousand people, called Duluth. Congressman Knott's speech would be filled with faulty facts and bad logic. But no matter. In an age of elaborate and energetic oratory it would be talked about, printed and reprinted, quoted and misquoted, for years to come.

According to the Congressional Globe, Knott was interrupted by "laughter," "great laughter," "roars of laughter," and "shouts of laughter" a total of sixty-two times. Once he had finished, the bill for the railroad was as dead as it could be, and he had made famous, by mistake, little Duluth, which the railroad never meant to put on the map in the first place. The speech immediately appeared in newspapers the country over and was published separately numerous times by private individuals. For several years it was handed out as a memento in the dining cars of the Northern Pacific Railroad. In the 1890's, by which time Duluth had become a city of thirty thousand people, the chamber of commerce published the speech to show that what had once been said "in ridicule and derision" had turned out to be facts "in reality." By the turn of the century the speech had appeared in at least three anthologies of American oratory.

As for J. (for James) Proctor Knott, he served two more terms in the House, later became governor of Kentucky, and spent his last years teaching economics and law at Centre College in Danville. Once he went to Duluth, to be received at a banquet in his honor. There were no hard feelings in "the Zenith City of the Unsalted Seas," as it was known by then. But never again did Knott reach the oratorical heights of the Duluth speech, which, perhaps to the detriment of his political career, left him marked as a humorist. Vice President Adlai Stevenson, whose grandson would experience a similar problem, wrote in his memoirs of Knott's extraordinary wit and his talents as a raconteur, describing an evening of yarn trading with Knott and Grover Cleveland, after which the President exclaimed, "It was a delight beyond compare." And another of Knott's comrades, the actor Joe Jefferson, said, "That man Knott is the greatest natural actor I have ever known; if he had gone on the stage he would have eclipsed us all."

Mathew Brady's portrait (page 79) suggests that Knott may have had difficulty eclipsing almost anyone. It was also charged, years after the speech, that Knott had had a ghost writer. The "evidence" was only that Knott never gave another speech that was anywhere near so funny. But if one were to judge Knott by the Duluth speech alone, which seems fair enough, his name deserves a place in history. It is also intriguing to imagine how he might eclipse some of the congressional spellbinders of our own day. After you have read his speech, imagine, for example, how J. Proctor Knott might address himself to the proposition of going to Mars or to the building of an s.s.t. There is every chance, of course, that he would be as mistaken about them as he was about Duluth; but certainly what he would do for the human spirit would be as welcome now as it was that January day a hundred years ago.

After addressing himself to the Speaker, Knott spent the first few minutes of his speech establishing a picture of the country through which the railroad was to pass, which he did mainly by quoting from previous testimony on the subject. The picture was one of bleak, sandy, godforsaken pinelands, which, he reminded his colleagues, one expert from Wisconsin had called "quite valueless." But all the same, Knott said he had nothing but the greatest enthusiasm for getting on with a railroad there, even though he had long had some doubts about the value of railroads in general. And then he commenced to explain why:

Years ago, when I first heard that there was somewhere in the vast *terra incognita*, somewhere in the bleak regions of the great Northwest, a stream of water known to the nomadic inhabitants of the neighborhood as the river St. Croix, I became satisfied that the construction of a railroad from that raging torrent to some point in the civilized world was essential to the happiness and prosperity of the American people, if not absolutely indispensable to the perpetuity of republican institutions on this continent. I felt instinctively that the boundless resources of that prolific region of sand and pine shrubbery would never be fully developed without a railroad constructed and equipped at the expense of the Government—and perhaps not then. I had an abiding presentiment that, some day or other, the people of this whole country, irrespective of party affiliations, regardless of sectional prejudices, and "without distinction of race, color, or previous condition of servitude," would rise in their majesty and demand an outlet for the enormous agricultural productions of those vast and fertile pine barrens, drained in the rainy season by the surging waters of the turbid St. Croix.

. . . Now, sir, who . . . who that is not as incredulous as St. Thomas himself, will doubt for a moment that the Goshen of America is to be found in the sandy valleys and upon the pine-clad hills of the St. Croix? Who will

About the time of J. Proctor Knott's speech in 1871, Duluth—unlike the "terrestrial paradise" he described—was a treeless, sidewalkless, muddy, and, to be generous, unattractive settlement on Lake Superior.

have the hardihood to rise in his seat on this floor and assert that, excepting the pine bushes, the entire region would not produce vegetation enough in ten years to fatten a grasshopper? Where is the patriot who is willing that his country shall incur the peril of remaining another day without the amplest railroad connection with such an inexhaustible mine of agricultural wealth? Who will answer for the consequences of abandoning a great and warlike people, in possession of a country like that, to brood over the indifference and neglect of their government? How long would it be before they would take to studying the Declaration of Independence and hatching out the damnable heresy of secession? How long before the grim demon of civil discord would rear again his horrid head in our midst, "gnash loud his iron fangs and shake his crest of bristling bayonets"?

. . . Now, sir, I repeat I have been satisfied for years that if there was any portion of the inhabited globe absolutely in a suffering condition for want of a railroad it was these teeming pine barrens of the St. Croix. At what particular point on that noble stream such a road should be commenced I knew was immaterial, and so it seems to have been considered by the draughtsman of this bill. It might be up at the spring or down at the foot log, or the water gate, or the fish dam, or anywhere along the bank, no matter where. But in what direction it should run, or where it should terminate, were always to my mind questions of the most painful perplexity. I could conceive of no place on "God's green earth" in such straitened circumstances for railroad facilities as to be likely to desire or willing to accept such a connection. . . .

Hence, as I have said, sir, I was utterly at a loss to determine where the terminus of this great and indispensable road should be, until I accidentally overheard some gentleman the other day mention the name of "Duluth." Duluth! The word fell upon my ear with peculiar and indescribable charm, like the gentle murmur of a low fountain stealing forth in the midst of roses, or the soft, sweet accents of an angel's whisper in the bright, joyous dream of sleeping innocence. Duluth! 'Twas the name for which my soul had panted for years, as the hart panteth for the water brooks. But where was Duluth? Never, in all my limited reading, had my vision been gladdened by seeing the celestial word in print. And I felt a profounder humiliation in my ignorance that its dulcet syllables had never before ravished my delighted ear. I was certain the draughtsman of this bill had never heard of it, or it would have been designated as one of the termini of this road. I asked my friends about it, but they knew nothing of it. I rushed to the Library and examined all the maps I could find. I discovered in one of them a delicate, hairlike line, diverging from the Missis-

sippi near a plàce marked Prescott, which I supposed was intended to represent the river St. Croix, but I could nowhere find Duluth.

Nevertheless, I was confident it existed somewhere, and that its discovery would constitute the crowning glory of the present century, if not of all modern times. I knew it was bound to exist in the very nature of things; that the symmetry and perfection of our planetary system would be incomplete without it, that the elements of material nature would long since have resolved themselves back into original chaos if there had been such a hiatus in creation as would have resulted from leaving out Duluth. In fact, sir, I was overwhelmed with the conviction that Duluth not only existed somewhere, but that wherever it was it was a great and glorious place. I was convinced that the greatest calamity that ever befell the benighted nations of the ancient world was in their having passed away without a knowledge of the actual existence of Duluth; that their fabled Atlantis, never seen save by the hallowed vision of inspired poesy, was, in fact, but another name for Duluth; that the golden orchard of the Hesperides was but a poetical synonym for the beer-gardens in the vicinity of Duluth. I was certain that Herodotus had died a miserable death because in all his travels and with all his geographical research he had never heard of Duluth. I knew that if the immortal spirit of Homer could look down from another heaven than that created by his own celestial genius upon the long lines of pilgrims from every nation of the earth to the gushing fountain of poesy opened by the touch of his magic wand, if he could be permitted to behold the vast assemblage of grand and glorious productions of the lyric art called into being by his own inspired strains, he would weep tears of bitter anguish that instead of lavishing all the stores of his mighty genius upon the fall of Ilion it had not been his more blessed lot to crystallize in deathless song the rising glories of Duluth. Yet, sir, had it not been for this map, kindly furnished me by the Legislature of Minnesota, I might have gone down to my obscure and humble grave in an agony of despair, because I could nowhere find Duluth. Had such been my melancholy fate, I have no doubt that with the last feeble pulsation of my breaking heart, with the last faint exhalation of my fleeting breath, I should have whispered, "Where is Duluth?"

But, thanks to the beneficence of that band of ministering angels who have their bright abodes in the far-off capital of Minnesota, just as the agony of my anxiety was about to culminate in the frenzy of despair, this blessed map was placed in my hands; and as I unfolded it a resplendent scene of ineffable glory opened before me, such as I imagine burst upon the enraptured vision of the wandering peri through the opening gates of paradise. There, there for the first time, my enchanted eye rested upon the ravishing word "Duluth."

This map, sir, is intended, as it appears from its title, to illustrate the position of Duluth in the United States; but if gentlemen will examine it, I think they will concur with me in the opinion that it is far too modest in its pretensions. It not only illustrates the position of Duluth in the United States, but exhibits its relations with all created things. It even goes further than this. It lifts the shadowy veil of futurity and affords us a view of the

*Sobersided though he seems in this Mathew Brady photograph, Knott brought down the House with allusions to Duluth's grandeur.*

golden prospects of Duluth far along the dim vista of ages yet to come.

If gentlemen will examine it they will find Duluth not only in the center of the map, but represented in the center of a series of concentric circles one hundred miles apart, and some of them as much as four thousand miles in diameter, embracing alike in their tremendous sweep the fragrant savannas of the sunlit South and the eternal solitudes of snow that mantle the icebound North. How these circles were produced is perhaps one of those primordial mysteries that the most skillful paleologist will never be able to explain. But the fact is, sir, Duluth

is preëminently a central place, for I am told by gentlemen who have been so reckless of their own personal safety as to venture away into those awful regions where Duluth is supposed to be that it is so exactly in the center of the visible universe that the sky comes down at precisely the same distance all around it.

I find by reference to this map that Duluth is situated somewhere near the western end of Lake Superior, but as there is no dot or other mark indicating its exact location I am unable to say whether it is actually confined to any particular spot, or whether "it is just lying around there loose." I really cannot tell whether it is one of those ethereal creations of intellectual frostwork, more intangible than the rose-tinted clouds of a summer sunset; one of those airy exhalations of the speculator's brain, which I am told are ever flitting in the form of towns and cities along those lines of railroad, built with Government subsidies, luring the unwary settler as the mirage of the desert lures the famishing traveler on, and ever on, until it fades away in the darkening horizon, or whether it is a real, bona fide, substantial city, all "staked off," with the lots marked with their owners' names, like that proud commercial metropolis recently discovered on the desirable shores of San Domingo.* But, however that may be, I am satisfied Duluth is there, or thereabout, for I see it stated here on this map that it is exactly thirty-nine hundred and ninety miles from Liverpool, though I have no doubt, for the sake of convenience, it will be moved back ten miles, so as to make the distance an even four thousand.

Then, sir, there is the climate of Duluth, unquestionably the most salubrious and delightful to be found anywhere on the Lord's earth. Now, I have always been under the impression, as I presume other gentlemen have, that in the region around Lake Superior it was cold enough for at least nine months in the year to freeze the smoke-stack off a locomotive. But I see it represented on this map that Duluth is situated exactly halfway between the latitudes of Paris and Venice, so that gentlemen who have inhaled the exhilarating airs of the one or basked in the golden sunlight of the other may see at a glance that Duluth must be a place of untold delights, a terrestrial paradise, fanned by the balmy zephyrs of an eternal spring, clothed in the gorgeous sheen of ever-blooming flowers, and vocal with the silvery melody of nature's choicest songsters. . . .

. . . As to the commercial resources of Duluth, sir, they are simply illimitable and inexhaustible, as is shown by this map. I see it stated here that there is a vast scope of territory, embracing an area of over two million square miles, rich in every element of material wealth and com-

*The annexation of Santo Domingo—now the Dominican Republic— to the United States, an idea championed by President Grant, was one of the major congressional issues of the day.

mercial prosperity, all tributary to Duluth. [Points to the map.] Look at it, sir. Here are inexhaustible mines of gold, immeasurable veins of silver, impenetrable depths of boundless forest, vast coal-measures, wide, extended plains of richest pasturage, all, all embraced in this vast territory, which must, in the very nature of things, empty the untold treasures of its commerce into the lap of Duluth.

Look at it sir, do not you see from these broad, brown lines drawn around this immense territory that the enterprising inhabitants of Duluth intend some day to enclose it all in one vast corral, so that its commerce will be bound to go there whether it would or not? And here, sir [still pointing to the map], I find within a convenient distance the Piegan Indians, which, of all the many accessories to the glory of Duluth, I consider by far the most inestimable. For, sir, I have been told that when the small-pox breaks out among the women and children of that famous tribe, as it sometimes does, they afford the finest subjects in the world for the strategical experiments of any enterprising military hero who desires to improve himself in the noble art of war, especially for any valiant lieutenant general whose

> *Trenchant blade, Toledo trusty,*
> *For want of fighting has grown rusty.*
> *And eats into itself for lack*
> *Of Somebody to hew and hack.*

. . . And here, sir, recurring to this map, I find in the immediate vicinity of the Piegans "vast herds of buffalo" and "immense fields of rich wheat lands."

*Here the hammer fell. Many cries: "Go on! Go on!"*

*The* SPEAKER. *Is there objection to the gentleman from Kentucky continuing his remarks? . . . The Chair hears none. The gentleman will proceed.*

MR. KNOTT. . . . I was remarking, sir, upon these vast "wheat fields" represented on this map in the immediate neighborhood of the buffaloes and the Piegans, and was about to say that the idea of there being these immense wheat fields in the very heart of a wilderness, hundreds and hundreds of miles beyond the utmost verge of civilization, may appear to some gentlemen as rather incongruous, as rather too great a strain on the "blankets" of veracity. But to my mind there is no difficulty in the matter whatever. The phenomenon is very easily accounted for. It is evident, sir, that the Piegans sowed that wheat there and plowed it with buffalo bulls. Now, sir, this fortunate combination of buffaloes and Piegans, considering their relative positions to each other and to Duluth, as they are arranged on this map, satisfies me that Duluth is destined to be the beef market of the world.

Here, you will observe [pointing to the map], are the buffaloes, directly between the Piegans and Duluth, and here, right on the road to Duluth, are the Creeks. Now, sir, when the buffaloes are sufficiently fat from grazing on those immense wheat fields you see it will be the easiest thing in the world for the Piegans to drive them on down, stay all night with their friends, the Creeks, and go into Duluth in the morning. I think I see them now, sir, a vast herd of buffaloes, with their heads down, their eyes glaring, their nostrils dilated, their tongues out, and their tails curled over their backs, tearing along toward Duluth, with about a thousand Piegans on their grass-bellied ponies, yelling at their heels! On they come! And as they sweep past the Creeks they join in the chase, and away they all go, yelling, bellowing, ripping, and tearing along, amid clouds of dust, until the last buffalo is safely penned in the stock-yards of Duluth!

Sir, I might stand here for hours and hours and expatiate with rapture upon the gorgeous prospects of Duluth, as depicted upon this map. But human life is too short and the time of this House far too valuable to allow me to linger longer upon the delightful theme. I think every gentleman on this floor is as well satisfied as I am that Duluth is destined to become the commercial metropolis of the universe, and that this road should be built at once. I am fully persuaded that no patriotic Representative of the American people, who has a proper appreciation of the associated glories of Duluth and the St. Croix, will hesitate a moment to say that every able-bodied female in the land between the ages of eighteen and forty-five who is in favor of woman's rights should be drafted and set to work upon this great work without delay. Nevertheless, sir, it grieves my very soul to be compelled to say that I cannot vote for the grant of lands provided for in this bill.

Ah! sir, you can have no conception of the poignancy of my anguish that I am deprived of that blessed privilege! There are two insuperable obstacles in the way. In the first place, my constituents, for whom I am acting here, have no more interest in this road than they have in the great question of culinary taste now perhaps agitating the public mind of Dominica, as to whether the illustrious commissioners who recently left this capital for that free and enlightened republic would be better fricasseed, boiled, or roasted, and in the second place these lands, which I am asked to give away, alas, are not mine to bestow! My relation to them is simply that of trustee to an express trust. And shall I ever betray that trust? Never, sir! Rather perish Duluth! Perish the paragon of cities! Rather let the freezing cyclones of the black Northwest bury it forever beneath the eddying sands of the raging St. Croix! ✪

conciliation succeed chastisement. . . ." But there was no persuading the majority; Chatham's appeal was rejected and the war went on unabated.

It began to appear, however, that destruction of the Continental Army—even if that goal could be achieved —might not be conclusive. After the disastrous campaign around Manhattan in 1776, George Washington had determined not to risk his army in a major engagement, and he began moving away from the European battle style in which two armies confronted each other head to head. His tactical method became that of the small, outweighed prizefighter who depends on his legs to keep him out of range of his opponent and who, when the bigger man begins to tire, darts in quickly to throw a quick punch, then retreats again. It was an approach to fighting described by Nathanael Greene, writing of the campaign in the South in 1780: "We fight, get beat, rise, and fight again." In fact, between January and September of the following year, Greene, short of money, troops, and supplies, won a major campaign without ever really winning a battle. The battle at Guilford Courthouse, which was won by the British, was typical of the results. As Horace Walpole observed, "Lord Cornwallis has conquered his troops out of shoes and provisions and himself out of troops."

There was, in the colonies, no great political center like Paris or London, whose loss might have been demoralizing to the Americans; indeed, Boston, New York, and Philadelphia, the seat of government, were all held at one time or another by the British without irreparable damage to the rebel cause. The fragmented political and military structure of the colonies was often a help to the rebels, rather than a hindrance, for it meant that there was almost no chance of the enemy striking a single crushing blow. The difficulty, as General Frederick Haldimand, who succeeded Carleton in Canada, saw it, was the seemingly unending availability of colonial militiamen who rose up out of nowhere to fight in support of the nucleus of regular troops called the Continental Army. "It is not the number of troops Mr Washington can spare from his army that is to be apprehended," Haldimand wrote, "it is the multitude of militia and men in arms ready to turn out at an hour's notice at the shew of a single regiment of Continental Troops. . . ." So long as the British were able to split up their forces and fan out over the countryside in relatively small units, they were fairly successful in putting down the irregulars' activities and cutting off their supplies; but the moment they had to concentrate again to fight the Continentals, guerrilla warfare burst out like so many small brush fires on their flank and rear. No British regular could tell if an American was friend or foe, for loyalty to King George was easy to attest; and the man who was a farmer or merchant when a British battalion marched by his home was a militiaman as soon as it had passed by, ready to shoulder his musket when an emergency or an opportunity to confound the enemy arose.

Against an unnumberable supply of irregular forces the British could bring to bear only a fixed quantity of troops—however many, that is, they happened to have on the western side of the Atlantic Ocean at any given moment. Early in the war General James Murray had foreseen the difficulties that would undoubtedly arise. Writing to Lord Barrington, he warned that military conquest was no real answer. If the war proved to be a long one, their advantage in numbers would heavily favor the rebels, who could replace their losses while the British could not. Not only did every musket and grain of powder have to be shipped across the ocean; but if a man was killed or wounded, the only way to replace him was to send another man in full kit across the Atlantic. And troop transports were slow and small: three or four were required to move a single battalion.

During the summer of 1775 recruiting went badly in England and Ireland, for the war was not popular with a lot of the people who would have to fight it, and there were jobs to be had. It was evident that the only means of assembling a force large enough to suppress the rebellion in the one massive stroke that had been determined upon was to hire foreign troops. And immediately this word was out, the rapacious petty princes of Brunswick, Hesse-Cassel, and Waldeck, and the Margrave of Anspach-Bayreuth, generously offered up a number of their subjects—at a price—fully equipped and ready for duty, to serve His Majesty George III. Frederick the Great of Prussia, seeing the plan for what it was, announced that he would "make all the Hessian troops, marching through his dominions to America, pay the usual cattle tax, because, although human beings, they had been sold as beasts." But George III and the princes regarded it as a business deal, in the manner of such dubious alliances ever since: each foot soldier and trooper supplied by the Duke of Brunswick, for instance, was to be worth seven pounds, four shillings, fourpence halfpenny in levy money to his Most Serene Highness. Three wounded men were to count as one killed in action, and it was stipulated that a soldier killed in combat would be paid for at the same rate as levy money. In other words the life of a subject was worth precisely seven pounds, four shillings, fourpence halfpenny to the Duke.

As it turned out, the large army that was assembled

in 1776 to strike a quick, overpowering blow that would put a sudden end to the rebellion proved—when that decisive victory never came to pass—to be a distinct liability, a hideously expensive and at times vulnerable weapon. In the indecisive hands of men like William Howe and Henry Clinton, who never seemed absolutely certain about what they should do or how they should do it, the great army rarely had an opportunity to realize its potential; yet, it remained a ponderous and insatiable consumer of supplies, food, and money.

The loyalists, on whom many Englishmen had placed such high hopes, proved a will-o'-the-wisp. Largely ignored by the policy makers early in the war despite their pleas for assistance, the loyalists were numerous enough but were neither well organized nor evenly distributed throughout the colonies. Where the optimists in Britain went wrong in thinking that loyalist strength would be an important factor was to imagine that anything like a majority of Americans *could* remain loyal to the Crown if they were not continuously supported and sustained by the mother country. Especially as the war went on, as opinions hardened, and as the possibility increased that the new government in America might actually survive, it was a very difficult matter to retain one's loyalty to the King unless friends and neighbors were of like mind and unless there was British force nearby to safeguard such a belief. Furthermore, it proved almost impossible for the British command to satisfy the loyalists, who were bitterly angry over the persecution and physical violence and robbery they had to endure and who charged constantly that the British generals were too lax in their treatment of rebels.

While the problems of fighting the war in distant America mounted, Britain found herself unhappily confronted with the combination of circumstances the Foreign Office dreaded most: with her armies tied down, the great European maritime powers—France and Spain—vengeful and adventurous and undistracted by war in the Old World, formed a coalition against her. When the American war began, the risk of foreign intervention was regarded as minimal, and the decision to fight was made on the premise that victory would be early and complete and that the armed forces would be released before any threatening European power could take advantage of the situation. But as the war continued without any definite signs of American collapse, France and Spain seized the chance to embarrass and perhaps humiliate their old antagonist. At first they supported the rebels surreptitiously with shipments of weapons and other supplies; then, when the situation appeared more auspicious, France in particular furnished active support in the form of an army and a navy, with catastrophic results for Great Britain.

One fascinating might-have-been is what would have happened had the Opposition in Parliament been more powerful politically. It consisted, after all, of some of the most forceful and eloquent orators imaginable, men whose words still have the power to send shivers up the spine. Not simply vocal, they were highly intelligent men whose concern went beyond the injustice and inhumanity of war. They were quick to see that the personal liberty of the King's subjects was as much an issue in London as it was in the colonies, and they foresaw irreparable damage to the empire if the government followed its unthinking policy of coercion. Given a stronger power base, they might have headed off war or the ultimate disaster; had the government been in the hands of men like Chatham or Burke or their followers, some accommodation with America might conceivably have evolved from the various proposals for reconciliation. But the King and North had the votes in their pockets, and the antiwar Opposition failed because a majority that was largely indifferent to reason supported the North ministry until the bitter end came with Cornwallis' surrender. Time and again a member of the Opposition would rise to speak out against the war for one reason or another: "This country," the Earl of Shelburne protested, "already burdened much beyond its abilities, is now on the eve of groaning under new taxes, for the purpose of carrying on this cruel and destructive war." Or, from Dr. Franklin's friend David Hartley: "Every proposition for reconciliation has so constantly and uniformly been crushed by Administration, that I think they seem not even to wish for the appearance of justice. The law of force is that which they appeal to. . . ." Or, from Sir James Lowther, when he learned that the King had rejected an "Olive Branch Petition" from the provincials: "Why have we not peace with a people who, it is evident, desire peace with us?" Or this, from General Henry Seymour Conway, inviting Lord North to inform members of the House of Commons about his overall program: "I do not desire the detail; let us have general outline, to be able to judge of the probability of its success. It is indecent not to lay before the House some plan, or the outlines of a plan. . . . If [the] plan is conciliation, let us see it, that we may form some opinion of it; if it be hostility and coercion, I do repeat, that we have no cause for a minute's consideration; for I can with confidence pronounce, that the present military armament will never succeed." But all unavailing, year after year, as each appeal to reason and humanity fell on ears deafened by self-righteousness and minds hardened against change.

Although it might be said that the arguments raised by the Opposition did not change the course of the war, they nevertheless affected the manner in which it was conducted, which in turn led to the ultimate British defeat. Whether Lord North was uncertain of that silent majority's loyalty is difficult to determine, but it seems clear that he was sufficiently nervous about public support to decide that a bold policy which risked defeats was not for him. As a result the war of the American Revolution was a limited war—limited from the standpoint of its objectives and the force with which Britain waged it.

In some respects the aspect of the struggle that may have had the greatest influence on the outcome was an intangible one. Until the outbreak of hostilities in 1775 no more than a small minority of the colonials had seriously contemplated independence, but after a year of war the situation was radically different. Now the mood was reflected in words such as these—instructions prepared by the county of Buckingham, in Virginia, for its delegates to a General Convention in Williamsburg: "... as far as your voices are admitted, you [will] cause a free and happy Constitution to be established, with a renunciation of the old, and so much thereof as has been found inconvenient and oppressive." That simple and powerful idea—renunciation of the old and its replacement with something new, independently conceived—was destined to sweep all obstacles before it. In Boston, James Warren was writing the news of home to John Adams in Philadelphia and told him: "Your Declaration of Independence came on Saturday and diffused a general joy. Every one of us feels more important than ever; we now congratulate each other as Freemen." Such winds of change were strong, and by contrast all Britain had to offer was a return to the status quo. Indeed, it was difficult for the average Englishman to comprehend the appeal that personal freedom and independence held for a growing number of Americans. As William Innes put it in a debate in Commons, all the government had to do to put an end to the nonsense in the colonies was to "convince the lower class of those infatuated people that the imaginary liberty they are so eagerly pursuing is not by any means to be compared to that which the Constitution of this happy country already permits them to enjoy."

With everything to gain from victory and everything to lose by defeat, the Americans could follow Livy's advice, that "in desperate matters the boldest counsels are the safest." Frequently beaten and disheartened, inadequately trained and fed and clothed, they fought on against unreasonably long odds because of that slim hope of attaining a distant goal. And as they fought on, increasing with each passing year the possibility that independence might be achieved, the people of Britain finally lost the will to keep going.

In England the goal had not been high enough, while the cost was too high. There was nothing compelling about the limited objective of bringing the colonies back into the empire, nothing inspiring about punishing the rebels, nothing noble in proving that retribution awaited

*The last boatload of the King's troops leaving the United States—New York, November 25, 1783*

those who would change the nature of things.

After the war had been lost and the treaty of peace signed, Lord North looked back on the whole affair and sadly informed the members of the House of Commons where, in his opinion, the fault lay. With a few minor changes, it was a message as appropriate to America in 1971 as to Britain in 1783: "The American war," he said, "has been suggested to have been the war of the Crown, contrary to the wishes of the people. I deny it. It was the war of Parliament. There was not a step taken in it that had not the sanction of Parliament. It was the war of the people, for it was undertaken for the express purpose of maintaining the just rights of Parliament, or, in other words, of the people of Great Britain, over the dependencies of the empire. For this reason, it was popular at its commencement, and eagerly embraced by the people and Parliament. . . . Nor did it ever cease to be popular until a series of unparalleled disasters and calamities caused the people, wearied out with almost uninterrupted ill-success and misfortune, to call out as loudly for peace as they had formerly done for war."

---

*Mr. Ketchum, senior editor of this company, is the author of our series of vignettes called* Faces from the Past *(recently published in book form under the same title). He was editor of* The American Heritage Book of the Revolution *and is currently writing a book about the crucial events of 1776, which he regards as the turning point of the struggle.*

*For further reading:* The British Empire Before the American Revolution, *Vol. 12,* The Triumphant Empire: Britain Sails into the Storm, 1770–1776, *by Lawrence Henry Gipson (Knopf, 1965);* British Politics and the American Revolution: The Path to War, 1773–75, *by Bernard Donoughue (St. Martin's Press, 1965);* The War for America, 1775–1783, *by Piers G. Mackesy (Harvard University Press, 1964);* The First Year of the American Revolution, *by Allen French (Octagon, 1967).*

# Which Way, America? CONTINUED FROM PAGE 13

(and, as anyone who heard his speeches will recall, the adjective was as important as the noun). One Washington correspondent privately referred to the Secretary as "a card-carrying Christian." Even before his untimely death in 1959 there were more than a few critics who argued that his militant anticommunism blinded him to changes in the Soviet world and condemned American diplomacy to a global rigidity. Yet to his many dedicated admirers, and especially to President Eisenhower, he was a man of principle and conscience, a Secretary of State who would never settle for a policy of expediency. Those

*Together in 1913, seated, left to right: Nataline Dulles, Mrs. John W. Foster, Eleanor Lansing Dulles, ex-Secretary John W. Foster, the John Foster Dulleses, Mrs. Robert Lansing. Standing are Kate and Emma Lansing and soon-to-be Secretary Lansing.*

who worked with him in the Cabinet or National Security Council were impressed with his almost total knowledge of all the facts in a given situation, his ability to present the relevant evidence, and his talent, as a lawyer, to write a brief resting upon seemingly irrefutable logic.

John Foster Dulles was, paradoxically, everything that both his critics and his admirers claimed. But he was, most emphatically, not simply one-dimensional; his personality had many and varied facets. A wide variety of experiences shaped the outlook and perspectives of this

complex man. His involvement in American foreign policy was, in many respects, the working out of a family drama. His grandfather (to whom he was particularly close) was John W. Foster, Secretary of State to Benjamin Harrison; his uncle, Robert Lansing, served Woodrow Wilson in the same capacity. Thus through family associations he gained an early exposure to the world of diplomacy and the workings of American foreign policy. He was also deeply affected by certain personal, firsthand experiences with the conduct of United States foreign policy from 1919 onward. Yet, despite his unique qualities and background, Dulles was a "typical" American in his response to the international issues that faced his country. The movement of his ideas was not far removed from the main currents of public opinion, except perhaps in the 1920's when he was more of an "internationalist" than all but a few of the surviving Wilsonians. Certainly in 1919 he was caught up in the general enthusiasm for the Wilsonian program, and, on the eve of World War II, he had no desire to see America involved. But once we were in it, he was again caught by the enthusiasm for internationalism and, like F.D.R., was hopeful that there could be postwar cooperation with the Soviet Union. Like most Americans, his suspicions of the Russians came largely after Yalta; they were founded on the disillusionment that arose when the wartime hopes were destroyed. Indeed, in the immediate postwar period, more than a few militant anti-Communists charged Dulles with not recognizing sufficiently the menace of the Soviets.

The purpose of the piece that follows is to illuminate some of the many facets of John Foster Dulles that have been noted in this brief introduction—above all, to suggest that he was far more complicated than the popular stereotype. It is based entirely upon two sources: first, his correspondence for the years 1919-1952, now on deposit in the Firestone Library of Princeton University; and second, transcripts of the Dulles Oral History Project, in the same library. The Oral History Project, directed by Philip Crowl, then of the Department of State and now chairman of the History Department at the University of Nebraska, taped the recollections of over three hundred persons who had known and worked with Dulles—Cabinet members, churchmen, colleagues in Wall Street and in the State Department, officers of the military services. They reveal aspects of the man not to be found in any letters or published sources. One cautionary note is in order. "Oral history" is not documented history; it rests on the fragile memories of men who, long after the fact, were asked to put their recollections on tape. The men cited in this article told it as they remembered it, not necessarily as it actually was.

John Foster Dulles was reared in Watertown, New York, where his father was pastor of the local Presbyterian church. Many years later his sister, Mrs. Margaret Edwards, recalled what it was like to grow up in a small town parsonage on the shores of Lake Ontario and what kind of boy her older brother had been:

He was an adventurous little boy. He wasn't foolhardy—never was—all his life. But he loved to climb the highest apple tree out in the back yard, and I would climb up after him as fast as I could. And when we shot off firecrackers on the Fourth of July, I just hated the noise, but I never let him know.

Our Sundays were quite strict, but they were happy days. In fact, I think we looked forward to Sundays. And every Sunday morning, as our family grew up, we five children, led by my mother, walked sedately up the church aisle and took our places next to the front pew. And each of us was equipped—this was my father's idea—with pencil and notebook. We were to take notes on the sermon. Of course, for the younger ones, my two little brothers, this didn't amount to very much. But for my brother Foster, and myself, and my brother Allen, it was a very serious undertaking. We felt that we were reporters on our father's sermon. And then at Sunday dinner our notes were brought forth, and we discussed the sermon. . . . My father would always say that if our notes were not clear, then he must have preached a very poor sermon. He always took the blame himself. So that made us very eager—because we loved our father—to make our notes as accurate as possible.

The family's intellectual horizons, however, were never limited to the view from the parsonage. Their father was, by the standards of nineteenth-century theology, a liberal; and he set broad educational goals for all the children—"being a world citizen, learning foreign languages, getting to know people face to face." To Mrs. Edwards, "all of those things that came out when Foster was Secretary of State . . . were all started by my father." Then, too, every year the Dulles children spent time in Washington visiting their grandfather, John W. Foster, no longer Secretary of State but still quite active in international affairs:

The Washington houses . . . were always centers of international personages, so that we kind of took that for granted. The Mexican ambassador lived next door, and the Chinese ambassador lived not far away . . . and they came and went from our house. My grandparents "received" every Monday, and, of course, social life and protocol was very detailed, and one made no mistakes . . . [Foster and I] would glue our faces to the windowpane to see these equipages roll up with their coachmen and their footmen, and then somebody would get out all dressed in regalia . . . so that I suppose it was in our blood when we were quite young.

It was a close-knit family, the children always in competition with one another but ever united against any outsider. Throughout their lives both Foster and Allen Dulles were resolute defenders of the family reputation. In the 1930's, for example, they edited the memoirs of their uncle, Robert Lansing and, in the opinion of the publisher, eliminated interesting but possibly unflattering material about Lansing's work with Woodrow Wilson. In a letter to his brother, Allen conceded having cut a section that "rather tended to indicate that Robert Lansing had been on the sidelines in connection with the preparation of the 14 Points message."

From Watertown High School, Foster Dulles went to Princeton, where he graduated in 1908. (The Princeton

U.P.I.

*More than six decades after the event, Secretary of State Dulles and Japanese Prime Minister Nobusuke Kishi admire a parchment painting showing the former's grandfather, Secretary of State John W. Foster, negotiating a treaty between Japan and China in 1895.*

record is obscure. Young Dulles was apparently a brilliant but shy and unsocial person; in later years few of his classmates could recollect much more than the fact that he had been with them at Princeton.) After college there was a year at the Sorbonne, with language study and philosophy courses under Henri Bergson, and then law school at George Washington University—so that he could be close to his grandfather. In 1913 Dulles joined the prestigious Wall Street law firm of Sullivan & Cromwell. There is more than a suspicion that it took the assistance of Grandfather Foster to land him his first job. As an old friend of the family later remembered:

Well, when he graduated, his grandfather, of course, wanted him to get a job so he brought him up to New York to Sullivan & Cromwell. And his grandfather knew Mr. Cromwell, and they had a meeting in Mr. Cromwell's office. And General Foster said, "Now, here is my grandson, just graduated from law school, so perhaps you could find a place for him." And Mlle. Reynard [Cromwell's secretary] said that Mr. Cromwell was so interested in the way Mr. Dulles behaved. This young man never raised his eyes from the floor. He was very shy, you know, at having his grandfather ask for a job rather than . . . getting it for himself.

Even in these years there were signs of an interest in international affairs. When his grandfather was named as one of the American delegates to the Second Hague Peace Conference in 1907, young Dulles accompanied him as his secretary. In 1913, when he was just beginning at Sullivan & Cromwell, Uncle Lansing tempted him with a chance to do some legal work for the State Department in Washington. In 1917–18, after America had gone to war and Dulles had temporarily left Wall Street for an Army commission, there were a few Lansing-inspired minor diplomatic missions to Central America. But Foster Dulles' first significant involvement with American foreign policy came in 1919 when he was a member of the American delegation in Paris to help Wilson write the Versailles Treaty.

Dulles worked on the issue of German reparations— how much Germany was to pay the victors for war damages—and, to his sorrow, lost many of the battles to keep the figures from being so high as to impede Germany's recovery. He was not alienated by the completed treaty. Throughout the twenties he continued to regard himself as a Wilsonian and moderate internationalist. But he was increasingly disturbed by the way in which the reparations question was handled.

Eustace Seligman, his law partner at Sullivan & Cromwell since prewar days, described the evolution of Dulles' attitude:

Dulles felt that the Versailles reparation burden on Germany was an impossible burden and would dislocate the economies of all the European countries. . . . Then, in 1939, he published a book in which he pointed out, without ever justifying any of their aggressions, that Germany, Italy, and Japan had been restricted in their economic and political development by French and British policies . . . and he advocated a recognition of the legitimacy of the demands of these countries—for which he was somewhat criticized.

All of this created a certain ambivalence in Dulles' attitude toward the rise of Adolf Hitler, as a letter he wrote to the editor of the *Forum* in 1937 indicates:

I am in receipt of your letter of September 20, with reference to

Professor [Emil] Ludwig's article on Hitler.
One may disagree, as I do, with many of Hitler's policies and methods. But such disagreement should not lead one into the error, as I conceive it, of disparaging his abilities. One who from humble beginnings, and despite the handicap of alien nationality, has attained the unquestioned leadership of a great nation cannot (as Ludwig maintains) have been "utterly lacking in talent, energy, and ideas." Professor Ludwig asserts that because Hitler's policies are blindly stupid, they are more apt than those of Mussolini to lead to war. This is a highly speculative prediction. . . . Admittedly Hitler's methods involve primarily an appeal to the emotions and the use of the arts of propaganda. Emotionalism is dangerous, whether in a people, a dictator, or an historian. But the user of emotional methods is not necessarily himself a mental incompetent.

As he became more involved in the arena of international finance, Dulles was a frequent speaker at business gatherings and at such organizations as the newly established Council on Foreign Relations. He was an internationalist by the standards of the 1920's; that is, he shared the view of many members of the Wall Street community with transatlantic financial interests, who felt that the United States, as the world's leading creditor nation, had a role to play in the world scene.

But in the late 1930's, as war shadows lengthened, Dulles became increasingly disillusioned about the state of international affairs. Believing, like a good Wilsonian, in the need for peaceful change, he insisted that another European conflict was threatening because no nation was prepared to live up to the implications of Article 19 of the Versailles Treaty, which had called for the revision of treaties that had become outmoded. He was wary of American involvement in such a struggle. When Charles A. Lindbergh began to emerge as the outspoken champion of isolationism, Dulles wrote him in guarded but sympathetic terms:

I am very glad you spoke as you did. I do not agree with everything that you said, but I do agree with the result, and I feel that there is grave danger that, under the influence of emotion, we will decide upon a national policy which is quite the reverse of what we had more or less agreed upon when we were thinking clearly.

The emotional reaction that Dulles feared was a commitment to defend democracy that might be impossible to fulfill. In the spring of 1940, he wrote to a friend advocating American assistance to Britain and France:

So far as Europe is concerned, I do not think there is anything we can do, or that any one can do, that will prevent the present war from impoverishing the nations of Europe and creating social and economic conditions such that a regime of personal and individual liberty, such as we aspire to, will be impracticable. This will, I fear, be true no matter who "wins."

And his concluding paragraph scarcely suggests the later

Secretary of State who would be accused of being an "immobilist" frozen into fixed positions:

If the defeat of England and France can only be prevented by the United States assuming the role of the guarantor of the *status quo* in Europe and Asia, then, indeed, we would have assumed a heavy responsibility. For, as I have said elsewhere, change is the one thing that cannot be permanently prevented, and the effort to perpetuate that which has become artificial will inevitably break the person or the nation committed thereto.

Yet in these same years, Foster Dulles, the son of a minister, began to find answers to pessimism in the peace efforts of American Protestantism. The year 1937 was crucial in his intellectual development. First, he attended an international conference on problems of war and peace that was held in Paris and sponsored by the League of Nations; then he crossed the Channel and attended a similar church-sponsored conference at Oxford. His son Avery recalled the contrast between the way his father responded to the two conferences:

In the summer of 1937, when he was in Paris . . . he had this great conference with many of the leading thinkers on financial and political matters in various countries. . . . But [he] . . . was rather dissatisfied with the results, because he felt that the people attending were not able to rise above their immediate national self-interest and prejudices. And then, right after it, he attended a conference of the Life and Work Group—which was one of these groups that later joined in the World Council of Churches—at Oxford on "Church, Community, and State." And he said that the atmosphere was so completely different when all these men were gathered together under Christian principles to discuss many of the same problems. He found that people of different nationalities were able to reach agreements transcending their short-term national self-interest and prejudices and see things in a much larger perspective. I think the contrast of these two conferences on world affairs in the summer of 1937 convinced him that Christianity was of tremendous importance for the solution of world problems of peace and international justice.

After 1937 Dulles plunged heavily into the work of the churches in world affairs, soon becoming a regular speaker at church-sponsored conferences and meetings on the problems of war and peace. His papers at Princeton contain an admiring note from his mother written about this time:

. . . just a few lines to tell you how much I appreciate what you are doing in the cause of Peace and Religion. I remember that after graduation [from college] when you told me that you were going into the law and not into the ministry, that you said that you thought you could do as much good in that field, and you are proving it, for your reputation gives weight to all you say.

Early in 1940, after the war had started in Europe, Dulles accepted the chairmanship of a major church-sponsored study group—the Commission on a Just and Durable Peace—established by the Federal Council of Churches. As head of that group Dulles became the lay spokesman for American Protestantism on the subject of war aims. Dulles and the commission insisted on the need to create a new international organization to replace the old League of Nations and, above all, hoped to establish a new international system that would create the possibility of peaceful change.

The churches, still smarting under charges that their outlook in the 1930's had been dominated by pacifism, found in Dulles a lay leader of conservative instincts and a Republican lawyer with impeccable credentials. He worked closely with some of the most liberal leaders of American Protestantism—men such as Reinhold Niebuhr and John Coleman Bennett—and, according to all accounts, was successful in the role. Bennett, later the president of Union Theological Seminary, recalled:

I should want to emphasize the fact that he was really the creative leader . . . the leader, indeed, of this effort for about a decade. He was, in dealing with these people, open, and he listened. . . . He always did his homework, he always had drafts, he always knew the line he wanted to take—a line having to do with the period after the war. . . . He was certainly opposed to a peace based primarily on a vindictive attitude—very open to the German people. And also, I thought, he was open toward the revolutionary part of the world to a considerable extent.

In the 1950's, when Dulles had become the alleged brinkman and advocate of massive retaliation, many church leaders looked back in some confusion. Was this the same Dulles with whom they had worked so closely during the war years? Former associates became critics, and there was strain in old relationships. In 1958 Dulles was asked to give a major speech at the annual meeting of the National Council of Churches in Cleveland. In it he insisted that the United States could not and should not give diplomatic recognition to Red China. He had scarcely returned to Washington when the five hundred delegates, by a wide margin, endorsed a resolution that called for U.N. recognition of the Red Chinese. Ernest Gross, a friend of the Secretary and a church delegate at Cleveland, recalled:

It [the vote] was strong and bitter medicine to Mr. Dulles, because word came back almost at once to us that he really felt it a personal blow and a repudiation.

But these discords were still in the future in the immediate postwar period, when Dulles clearly emerged into national prominence as an authority on American foreign policy. In both the 1944 and 1948 election campaigns he was Thomas E. Dewey's principal consultant on foreign affairs. Indeed, in 1948, on that historic occasion when Dewey (the Republican candidate) "snatched defeat from the jaws of victory," it was widely assumed that Dulles would be the next Secretary of State. All of this caused no little embarrassment. At the time of the election Dulles was in Paris attending a meeting of the U.N. General Assembly, and as the Israeli foreign minister, Abba Eban, recalled the circumstances:

At that time, in the early part of November and late October, everybody in Paris who talked to Dulles assumed that he was talking to the prospective Secretary of State, and all sorts of dinner parties and meetings were held on this assumption, which nobody questioned at the time. Dulles himself was inviting delegates and groups of delegates to have dinner, during

*"You Sure Everything's All Right, Foster?"*
Herblock's Here and Now (SIMON & SCHUSTER, 1955)

which he would lay down future lines of policy. It fell to me to be invited on November 4, the day after the election, and the occasion had all the melancholy of a funeral . . .

Dulles' stature was enhanced by his position as delegate at several U.N. General Assembly meetings. He became both an official and unofficial Republican adviser to the Department of State. He was asked to negotiate and carry through the Japanese Peace Treaty. The important aspect of the years from 1948 to 1952, however, was the change in his views toward the Soviet Union and his emergence as one of the architects of the postwar bipartisan foreign policy of containment and resistance. Dulles was relatively slow to emerge as a militant anti-Communist; throughout the late 1940's he continued to

express fears about the global spread of American commitments, worried about the fragmentation of the United Nations, and on occasion doubted whether the East-West split was irrevocable. On the very eve of Truman's enunciation of the Truman Doctrine, Dulles wrote Joseph Barnes of the New York *Herald Tribune:*

I read with great interest your piece in today's "Tribune." I am in general agreement with it except that I do not feel that the Soviet ideological challenge "would prove embarrassing and costly to us even if it never produced a war." My personal feeling is that, if the Soviet challenge does not produce a war, and I think it will not, it may prove to be a useful and invigorating thing. I do not know whether you are familiar with Toynbee's story of History and his study of the rise and fall of civilizations in terms of "challenge and response." Without periodic challenge it seems that civilizations decline and pass away.

In 1952 Dulles emerged as Eisenhower's choice for Secretary of State. The two men, however, scarcely knew each other until the spring of that year, when a carefully planned meeting was arranged in Paris so that they could sound each other out and determine if they could work together. It had always been assumed by those who knew Dulles that, consciously or unconsciously, he had always sought the position of Secretary of State. Yet when the first overtures came from Dwight Eisenhower's camp, Dulles had hesitations. His long-time partner, Eustace Seligman, remembered what happened when Lucius Clay, who handled the arrangements, first called:

I remember I went up to Foster's room and asked if he could go over to Paris the next week and told him what it was about. Foster got another of our partners, Arthur Dean, and the three of us discussed it. And this is something that people I've told it to don't believe. Foster said, "I don't think I really want to become Secretary of State." And the reason was, he didn't want the administrative detail. He didn't want the political business of having to go up to the Hill to persuade people. He said, "The job I would like to have would be head of the planning group—to plan foreign policy and not to have to worry about these other unimportant things."

Dulles, quite obviously, resolved his doubts, realizing that he would not have the necessary authority or control without the actual position as Secretary of State. To be sure, he never really "ran" the State Department in any full managerial sense; he administered, as Robert Murphy, a career diplomat who had worked with Eisenhower since the North African invasion in 1942, put it, "sporadically." Moreover, though he and the President eventually established a close and personal relationship, at the outset of the new administration there were those who thought the two men were incompatible and who wondered if Dulles would survive as Secretary for even a year. Emmet John Hughes, journalist and speechwriter for the administration, insisted that in the early days of the Eisenhower-Dulles association the President was "just plain bored" by his new appointee:

It was so emphatic and obvious a boredom that I found it embarrassing, even though I was not terribly sympathetic to Foster Dulles . . . I recall, too, that after some of these rather long conferences broke up, during which the President-elect would just stare up at the ceiling as if in a trance every time Foster Dulles talked, C. D. Jackson and I would remark on this, and we both had identical reactions to the phenomenon. We both reached the conclusion, that would seem to be inescapable, that this was a human relationship that could not endure.

In later years the Eisenhower temper flashed when he was questioned about the accuracy of Hughes's observations: "That's a complete distortion of fact. Matter of fact, the man [Hughes] knew nothing about it. How did he know what my reactions were? Matter of fact, I admired Dulles from the very beginning . . ." But others also noted the roughness in the early relationship of President and Secretary. Robert Murphy was forcibly struck by the difference between the way Dulles and Walter B. Smith, the new Undersecretary of State, approached the President (General Smith had been Eisenhower's Chief of Staff at SHAEF during the war):

He'd [Smith] call up on the phone . . . or the President would call him, and he'd say, "Ike, I think you ought to do this" or "I think that's a hell of a thing. Don't do that." . . . Then I'd go from Smith's office, maybe, to Dulles' office, and Dulles would be on the phone to the President, and he'd be all deference and politeness, and "Mr. President," and there was no informality there.

Like many of the newcomers Dulles apparently feared that many officials of the State Department had been corrupted and brainwashed by twenty years of service to Democratic administrations. In his first talk to members of the department he called for a new regime of "positive loyalty," and, as Douglas MacArthur II recalled the incident, thereby alienated many with whom he would have to work:

He addressed the Foreign Service and the State Department shortly after he took over, and he presented his remarks in a way which was interpreted by many . . . to have cast some doubt on their loyalty to the government. It was one of those things where the Secretary did not have a text, and I think he could have said what he had to say and put it in a different way . . .

A strained atmosphere was also created by the feeling of many in the State Department that Dulles was willing to tolerate right-wing attacks on alleged "subversives" in their ranks and to appease the congressional followers of Communist-hunting Senator Joseph R. McCarthy. "There was quite a bit of feeling in the Foreign Service," Theodore Achilles noted, "that he was not standing up

strongly in the defense of some people, including Chip Bohlen, who was the most prominent case at that time and who was under attack by McCarthy." The recollections of Edward Corsi, New York State commissioner of labor, were bitter. Corsi, a liberal Republican, was invited to take on a State Department assignment handling refugee problems, but he had scarcely arrived in Washington before he came under intense attack from the House Un-American Activities Committee for alleged Communist sympathies. As the furor mounted, suggestions were made to Corsi that the best way out was for

"Don't Be Afraid—I Can Always Pull You Back"
Herblock's Special For Today (SIMON & SCHUSTER, 1958)

him to resign his post in Washington and, in its place, accept "a roving ambassadorship in Latin America." Corsi flatly rejected this "solution" and sought a personal meeting with Dulles:

Finally, I couldn't take it. I had to have a showdown with John Foster Dulles himself. . . . My house was filled with reporters and people trying to create this into a huge national scandal of some kind. . . . I had to get a clearance from the Secretary one way or the other.

I went there at four o'clock. Of course downstairs was just packed up with dozens of photographers. . . . I ducked them and got into the Secretary's office. . . . He sat there. He looked like a beaten man. It seemed that the tragedy was more his than mine. And he said, "You know, Ed, we have to depend on Congress for our appropriations."

"Very true, Mr. Secretary," I said. "What is the meaning of this? Do you want me to leave?"

"No," he said, "no, Ed, why don't you accept [the ambassadorship]?" I said, "Because I'm not interested in that offer."

Then he went off into a spiel about what these same elements had done to him on the Hiss case. And he said, "Don't you know that I went through this kind of thing with all these people? You can't pacify these people; there's no reasoning with [them]. They've got the cards in their hands. They can stop our appropriations. They can do a great many things." And so on.

I realized, the more I talked, the more I was dealing with a man who was determined to put an end to this thing, and the way to put an end to it was to run away from it.

These incidents, to be sure, occurred early in the new administration, at a time when things often go wrong for Washington newcomers. With the passage of time many of these problems were solved, sorted out, or simply shelved. With the fall of Senator McCarthy the attack on the State Department waned, and departmental morale improved. Dulles himself gained increased respect for the Foreign Service. His relationship with the President firmed; indeed, it became exceptionally close. Emmet Hughes, returning to the White House in 1956, found a harmony he had never expected. President Eisenhower later recalled that "there were so many telephone calls with Dulles, that you just didn't attempt to keep track of the number. I'd just reach for the phone myself and call, and he'd do the same thing. . . . We'd be in close touch all the time. I suppose some days eight or ten times . . . I'd call him, or he'd drop in, or send somebody over, just for a few moments about something. . . . But always—I suppose there was no one I kept in as close touch with as I did with Foster."

All of this was to the occasional annoyance of Sherman Adams, the granite Cerberus from New Hampshire, whose task it was to guard access to Dwight Eisenhower. Adams was devoted to keeping the President's schedule "orderly," a chore made all the more difficult because, in his words, Eisenhower was "a friendly man who would have welcomed all":

Dulles was the only member of the Cabinet who took literally Ike's invitation to come in any time and, when not occupied, simply to walk in. Dulles would walk in here, ask Shanley, Stevens, etc. if the President was busy, and, if not, Dulles just opened the door and walked in.

Once, Adams barred Gerard Smith, Dulles' adviser on nuclear matters and disarmament, from a White House meeting despite Smith's insistence that Dulles had sent him over as his personal representative. Said Smith:

. . . I went back and reported the thing . . . to Foster. And then he said, "You know, Gerry, Adams talks to me that way sometimes." And then he added, "But not very often."

Dulles soon established himself, in both the Cabinet and National Security Council, as one of the most influential and respected members of the administration. His reputation was based upon his mastery of facts and detail, his total command of every aspect of a problem under discussion, his ability to marshal evidence and mount his case. The laconic Sherman Adams was eloquent on the point:

There were occasions, when, at the Cabinet table, Mr. Dulles really took his hair down. . . . Although he would not show impatience toward some remark which Mr. [Ezra] Benson or some other member of the Cabinet would make, he nevertheless occasionally gave the Cabinet a—well, I thought they were grand lectures. He would start with the various elements that made up a situation with which we were faced, to look at the alternatives, and so unmistakenly bring the Cabinet to a conclusion that he really took Mr. Humphrey and some of the others into camp.

What impressed General Matthew Ridgway, himself no stranger to professional briefings, about Dulles' presentations in the National Security Council was his "ability to take the whole complex international situation and, in the course of fifteen or twenty minutes . . . brief the NSC without a note before him, in a most lucid manner, with beautiful continuity. It was a really marvelous display of intellect and memory and grasp of the whole situation."

It was quite simple to Dwight Eisenhower:

I admired the man from the very beginning for two reasons. One, his obvious sincerity and dedication to the problems that were put before him, and secondly, the orderliness of his mind. He had a little habit before he started to speak—probably in his youth, he may have had a little bit of stammering—he waited, sometimes it would be three or four seconds, before he'd start to talk. But when he did, it was almost like a printed page.

There was also a certain ineffable quality about Dulles that made him both the spokesman for and symbol of the foreign policies of the Eisenhower administration. It was his successor, Christian Herter, the gentle man from Massachusetts, who most clearly sensed this quality:

The major differences between ourselves was my own feeling that the President was the constitutional officer responsible for foreign affairs. Whether he made the policy, or didn't make the policy, he still ought to be out in front in connection with it. I didn't want it to be known as a Herter policy; I'd much rather have it an Eisenhower policy . . . [pause] . . . I think Foster rather liked it being a Dulles policy.

Whether it was a strength or a weakness, the "lawyer's mind" of Dulles can readily be detected in many of his policies. SEATO, for example, was deliberately designed to meet a series of constitutional, political, and legal problems far more than it was intended to be simply a military alliance on the NATO model. Richard Bissell, deputy director of the CIA, insisted that it was a lawyer's and not a soldier's concept. Recalling the occasion when Dulles first discussed the idea for SEATO, Bissell emphasized that the Secretary had placed great stress upon the factors that had prevented American intervention in Indochina when the French position collapsed in 1954 and also had made it clear that he did not expect the nations of Southeast Asia to provide any appreciable military power or political stability to the proposed treaty:

Dulles made a great deal of the fact that the circumstances which had tied our hands at the time of Dien Bien Phu and [prevented] a possible direct military intervention, were in part the lack of a position in international law which would justify an intervention and in part a domestic constitutional problem. . . . Dulles argued at the meeting . . . that an appropriate regional treaty in Southeast Asia would have, in effect, made possible the overcoming of these legal obstacles to military intervention in the area should we ever be faced with a situation in which that might be necessary. In the first place, as a treaty it would have been debated in the Congress and ratified by the Senate. Therefore, in its domestic aspect, this would be a legislative action with a legislative history that would clearly augment Presidential powers to react quickly. . . .

Internationally the point was more obvious that if a government in the area required our assistance, the treaty would provide a recognized . . . legal basis for rendering such assistance.

But if colleagues saw the lawyer dominant, many also saw the Presbyterian moralist rampant. He was, to them, the churchman in politics whose religious rejection of "atheistic communism" made him identify the Soviets and their allies with the forces of evil. Roscoe Drummond, the New York *Herald Tribune*'s man in Washington, noted the prevailing view among the press corps that "Dulles wrapped his temporal views in theological clothes in a way that made him seem smug and moralistic." Even his friends noted the same quality. To James Hagerty, the President's press secretary:

Dulles was a tough old boy. . . . He was a Roundhead, a Puritan, and I'm quite sure that in the Cromwell era his ancestors were chopping down the Cavaliers in the name of their religious beliefs.

Christian Herter made the same point, but in different language:

I think that you have to give some allowance to the fact that Foster was essentially a very religious person, and I think that the very thought of communism, and the ungodliness of communism . . . was something he felt very deeply inside.

A senior American diplomat, the late George V. Allen, long remembered an evening when he was a guest in the Dulles home. During the after-dinner conversation, Allen made a few unflattering comments about the democratic leadership provided by Syngman Rhee and Chiang Kai-shek. Dulles leaned forward in his chair, and, as Allen recalled it, his eyes were blinking:

Well, I'll tell you this. No matter what you say about them, these two gentlemen are modern-day equivalents of the founders of the church. They are Christian gentlemen who have suffered for their faith. They have been steadfast and have upheld the faith . . .

At a meeting in the State Department, someone once made a Biblical reference. The Secretary waved his finger and, as Robert Murphy recalled, said, "I want it understood that I know more about the Bible than anybody else in this Department." Gerard Smith had a firsthand experience with that knowledge. He was on a transatlantic flight with Dulles and working on a speech that the Secretary was to deliver concerning the state of NATO. Unwisely, as it turned out, Smith decided to include a Biblical quotation, "When a strong man is armed, his castle is in peace":

I handed Dulles the manuscript, and he called me to the back of the plane and said, "Where did you get this quote?" And I told him, and he said, "Well, is there a Bible aboard?" And I dug into the reference books and found a Bible, and pointed out the passage. He looked and looked at it.

Finally, the next day he called me in and said—he knew that I was a Roman Catholic—"What do your theologians say is the meaning of that passage? . . . My sense of it is that this is a reference to Satan."

So I called up someone learned in the New Testament and recited it to him—"When a strong man is armed, his castle is in peace." I said, "Who does this refer to?" He replied, "Why, Satan, of course. . . . Look at the next line, for it says, 'But when a stronger man comes, he overcomes him'—and that's the reference to Christ."

Well, I went shamefacedly to Dulles. He got a great kick out of it. "Just think what my Presbyterian friends would have said, if they heard me saying that to the country at large."

Yet those who saw only the stern face of the Secretary on TV or who knew him only for his incantations about the evils of communism were unaware that the Secretary was also a man with a sense of humor and kindness. Behind the preaching of the brinkman there was warmth of personality.

Thomas Gates, Undersecretary of the Navy, remembered the first time he and his wife attended an official Washington dinner party at which the Secretary of State was present. Mrs. Gates, apprehensive that she would be seated next to the austere Dulles, found that he was indeed her dinner partner:

And she sat down, and Dulles started to pull the candle grease off the candles and eat it. . . . And my wife said, "Now, Mr. Dulles." He said, "I know it's awful, it's a terrible habit, but I just love to chew candle grease. I've done it all my life." My wife said, "Well, you shouldn't do it. I've scolded my children all their lives, and it messes up the tablecloth." And he laughed, and they got along swimmingly.

Well, my wife went out and bought two boxes of those bee's honey candles that are made out in San Diego in some missionary place and sent them up to his camp in the Thousand Islands. And she got back a letter which she thinks is the greatest letter she's ever had. It said, "Dear Mrs. Gates: The candles arrived. They look good, they light good, and they chew good."

One Saturday the Secretary was about to depart on one of his frequent trips abroad. He and Douglas MacArthur II spent most of the day working on papers they would have to take with them. Around midafternoon Dulles announced that he was going home and would meet MacArthur at the airport at nine in the evening. "And I want you to go home, too," he told MacArthur, "and see something of your family before we're off tonight. And that's an order." MacArthur promised to quit in a few more minutes, though, knowing how much work still remained to be done, he had no intention of leaving. He kept on sorting papers. About 6:30 the phone rang:

I was feeling tired, and when the phone rang, I said, "Yeah, who's this?"

And this voice replied, "This is Dulles. You better go home, boy. Your home front is crumbling . . . I mean it. You go home right away."

So, I immediately hung up the phone and called my wife. I said, "I'll be home in about an hour to pick up my clothes. But I just got this strange phone call from the Secretary. Do you know what it's all about?" And I repeated what he said to me.

My wife said, "Yes, I do know what it's all about. About fifteen minutes ago, the telephone rang, and a voice said, 'I want to speak to Mr. MacArthur.'"

And she said, "Who's calling please?" And this voice replied, "Secretary Dulles."

My wife, thinking it was one of the Secretary's minions, said in a rather hard voice, "Well, you go back and tell the Secretary that Douglas MacArthur is where he is every Saturday, every Sunday, every night. He's down in that damned State Department."

The voice replied with a chuckle, "I will give that message to the Secretary." Of course it was the Secretary himself.

Two phrases—"brinkmanship" and "massive retaliation"—will long be irrevocably associated with John Foster Dulles. Both were controversial and, as shorthand, capsule statements of complex policies, helped to create the image of Dulles as the dogmatist who revelled in the confrontation between East and West. Ernest Gross was present when the "massive retaliation" speech was given before the Council on Foreign Relations on January 12, 1954, and remembered the negative impact it made on him and many other council members:

A group of council members went to the hotel bar afterwards. And really we all expressed a sense of shock and consternation at that speech. A group of really knowledgeable people gathered afterwards, and we all shook our heads and were really worried.

In this speech, as in many others, Dulles was his own worst enemy. He sincerely desired to communicate his ideas to the American public and thereby secure broad acceptance of administration policies. But to command attention he often used dramatic, abbreviated phrases—and failed to realize that these could be counterproductive. Robert Bowie, twice member of the Policy Planning Staff, noted the ironies emerging from the massive-retaliation speech:

I am quite certain that Dulles' concepts . . . assumed the capacity for more limited force. In private discussion he would always express the view that there must be an opportunity for a flexible use of force, and not simply one choice. . . . But in speaking he was so anxious to get things clear and simple and forceful and to have them get attention, that he gave the picture of a mind that had all . . . the qualities of simplification in black and white.

Much the same thing happened with respect to the equally famous "brinkmanship" article that appeared in *Life* magazine in January of 1956 and that rounded out the impression of Dulles as a man who was sufficiently bellicose to atomize large portions of the globe on less-than-massive provocation. The article, "Three Times to the Brink," was based on a tape recording that Dulles made with three journalists who worked for various Luce publications. On the actual tape Dulles had been trying to explain why, in his opinion, a nation confronted with a grave crisis and dealing with a remorseless enemy could not, in advance, afford to indicate that it would yield to pressure. To do so, Dulles argued, might tempt the enemy to press too far, to assume that the nation lacked will, and therefore, to miscalculate—thereby actually increasing the prospect of war. But in taping his remarks the Secretary had used such phrases as "the ability to get to the verge of war without getting into war as the necessary art," had talked about not being "scared to go to the brink," and had described President Eisenhower as "coming up taut" on several crucial decisions. No journalist could resist the potential in such copy, and *Life* further compounded the problem by tightening the piece, inserting provocative subheads, and adding the title "Three Times to the Brink" on the cover. James Shepley, who wrote the article on the basis of the Dulles tape, admitted:

We had committed the sin of oversensationalizing what he had said at that point. . . . Because of the way we headlined and covered the thing, it was readily subject to the misinterpretation that . . . he appeared to be bragging about taking the country to the brink of war.

Henry Luce, publisher of *Life* and long an admirer of Dulles, said:

Shepley's mistake was putting something in quotation marks which should not have been put in quotation marks. . . . He should have . . . given the sense of the thing—and the sense of the thing was that in very tense world affairs, there are times when you have to be willing to go to the brink of war. You can't carry out your policy without any risk of war whatever. . . . But Dulles had put this a little dramatically in saying, "going to the brink."

Two men—Richard Nixon and Dwight Eisenhower—admired Dulles almost beyond all others. To Nixon the great strength of the Secretary was his firmness and, above all, his willingness to pursue a policy that he felt was correct even though unpopular:

So, let me put it this way: some political leaders in the decision-making process would put their finger in the air and say, What do people want? Dulles never believed in decision-making by Gallup Poll. . . . He said, "After all, you don't take a Gallup Poll to find out what you ought to do in Nepal. Most people don't know where Nepal is, let alone most Congressmen and Senators. But what you do is to determine what policy should be, and then if there's a controversy and if there's need for public understanding, you educate the public."

Richard Nixon also felt a personal debt to Dulles for the assistance that the Secretary gave him in 1955, when President Eisenhower suffered his heart attack and the young Vice President was thrust into a position of both national leadership and vulnerability. On this occasion the wheel came full circle. Dulles, the nephew of Robert Lansing, could draw on family experience in the matter of Presidential disability and had strong views about what had gone wrong when Woodrow Wilson was struck down in 1919. In Nixon's words:

Basically, there had to be, at that time, some one on whom I could rely . . . Dulles was one—he was the first. Dulles was the one who, because of the accident that he had been through it before with his uncle, advised me and guided me. [He] was my major adviser as to what I should do and the role that I should play. And he was also the one that urged Sherman Adams to go out to Denver so that we would not have the Wilson experience of just Mrs. Eisenhower and a press secretary out there. . . . He also urged that Cabinet meetings be held, and that the National Security Council meetings be held, and that the President write me a note—in fact, I would say that Dulles was really the general above all at that point. Others contributed to what we ought to do, but we never did anything in that period without checking it with Dulles.

The man whom Dwight Eisenhower remembered was the man of moral principle:

Not only were our relations very close and cordial, but on top of that I always regarded him as an assistant and an associate with whom I could talk things out very easily, digging in all their various facets and tangents—and then, when a final decision was made, I could count on him to execute them. . . . On top of that, the man was possessed of a very strong faith in moral law. And, because of that, he was constantly seeking what was right, and what conformed to the principles of human behavior as we'd like to believe them and see them. . . .

And it was a tremendously serious blow to me when that second operation showed that Foster was filled up with cancer. I not only liked the man—and I just hated to think of going on without his brain—but it's one of those things fate brings along and you have to learn to live with it.

Wiley Buchanan, chief of protocol in the State Department, handled the funeral arrangements when John Foster Dulles died in the spring of 1959:

The first time I was in the President's office after the funeral, I started out the door, and he said, "Wiley, come back here for a minute." I went over by the window, looking out at the lawn of the White House—out of his oval office. And he said, "I just wanted to thank you and your people for arranging the funeral. It couldn't have been better, and I was well pleased with it." Then he lowered his eyes, and, actually, tears filled them, and he said, "It's a great loss."

---

*Professor Richard Challener, of Princeton University, is a specialist in modern American diplomatic and military history. John Fenton, a former editor with the Gallup Poll, works in Princeton's Office of Public Information. They are writing a biography of John Foster Dulles to be published by Harper & Row.*

*The public hardly ever saw the Dulles who relaxed with friends, as shown here in 1958. Though in a rare moment of rest, his drawn face shows signs of the illness that was fatal the next year.*

# Arnhem

CONTINUED FROM PAGE 63

was to be coordinated with a "rapid and violent" thrust by a British armored column along the Arnhem highway.

Previous airborne operations had shown that the effectiveness of paratroops varied in inverse proportion to the time they had to hold their objectives; in a long fight they were invariably overmatched in firepower. On the face of it, then, laying down a carpet of paratroopers and glider-borne infantry up to sixty-five miles ahead of the ground forces, as Market-Garden proposed to do, was a very high-risk tactic. Eisenhower and Montgomery counted on the condition of the German forces in Holland to even the odds. Allied intelligence was confident that behind a thin crust of resistance along the Meuse-Escaut Canal, there was hardly any organized enemy at all.

Opposing the Allies in this northern sector was Field Marshal Walther Model, working with his characteristic furious energy to patch together a defensive line. Model was a stocky, roughhewn character, a favorite of Hitler's who had performed well in crises on the Eastern Front and who liked to call himself "the *Führer's* Fireman." His command had been so badly shattered in France, however, that facing Montgomery in early September there was only a mixed bag of stragglers, garrison troops, and *Luftwaffe* ground units, braced by a few green paratroop regiments and some fanatical but inexperienced SS men. Line infantry and armor were in very short supply.

A few days before Market-Garden was scheduled to begin, fragmentary reports came in from the Dutch underground of two German armored formations that had just bivouacked north of Arnhem, apparently for refitting. Allied intelligence surmised that these must be the 9th and 10th SS Panzer divisions. Both were known to have been decimated in the French debacle, and intelligence discounted them as a threat to the operation.

In England U.S. Lieutenant General Lewis H. Brereton's First Allied Airborne Army, honed to a fine edge, was spoiling for a fight. The three divisions slated for Market-Garden—the U.S. 82nd and 101st Airborne, veterans of the Normandy airdrop, and the 1st British Airborne, which had fought in Sicily and Italy—had seen eighteen scheduled drops cancelled in a period of forty days as the ground forces advanced too fast to need them.

The mission of Maxwell Taylor's 101st Airborne was a drop near Eindhoven to seize that city and key river and canal bridges. Farther along the road to Arnhem would be James Gavin's 82nd Airborne, assigned the big bridges over the Maas at Grave and over the Waal at Nijmegen, plus a ridge line to the east that dominated both bridges.

The farthermost objective, the bridge over the Lower Rhine at Arnhem, was allotted to Robert E. Urquhart's 1st British Airborne, assisted by a brigade of Polish paratroops.

In tactical command was British Lieutenant General Frederick Browning, dapper and brusque, the husband of novelist Daphne du Maurier. Browning had his reservations about the operation. Montgomery assured him he had to hold the Arnhem airhead only two days. "We can hold it for four," Browning replied. "But I think we might be going a bridge too far."

The ground forces, led by the Guards Armoured Division of the British Second Army, were to begin their northward push as the airdrop began. In command was Brian Horrocks, tall and white-haired and with something of the manner of a Biblical prophet about him. He had served Montgomery in North Africa and was both energetic and capable. Unlike Browning, Horrocks radiated optimism about the speed his forces would make. "You'll be landing on top of our heads," he warned the paratroops in mock seriousness.

Market-Garden lacked the "tidiness"—a substantial margin of superiority—that Montgomery usually demanded in an operation. There were few reserves in case of trouble and, with Patton embroiling the Third Army in battle to the south to keep his supplies coming, only minimum supporting stocks of gasoline and ammunition. Nevertheless, the plan was bold and imaginative; if the Germans were indeed on the brink of collapse, a victory at Arnhem just might provide the extra shove to keep the pursuit rolling and measurably shorten the war.

The opening phase of the largest airborne operation in history was, in the words of an RAF pilot, "a piece of cake." D-day, September 17, 1944, was clear and windless, ideal for an airdrop. Shortly before 1 P.M.—following a softening-up of German defenses by 1,400 Allied bombers—some 1,400 transport planes and 425 gliders, plus swarms of escorting fighters, blackened the skies over Holland.

Edward R. Murrow had wangled a place in one of the 101st Airborne's C-47's to make a recording of his impressions for CBS Radio. "Now every man is out . . .," Murrow reported. "I can see their chutes going down now . . . they're dropping beside the little windmill near a church, hanging there, very gracefully, and seem to be completely relaxed, like nothing so much as khaki dolls hanging beneath green lampshades. . . . The whole sky is filled with parachutes."

On the ground below, a few miles from the 101st's drop zones, German General Kurt Student watched the sight with frank envy. Student was a pioneer of airborne warfare who had led the aerial assaults on Rotterdam and Crete. "How I wish that I had ever had such a powerful force," he remarked wistfully to an aide. Dutch civilians returning from church cheered the awesome sight. As the paratroopers landed, the Dutch rushed out to meet them with offers of food from their Sunday tables.

Max Taylor's 101st Airborne in the Eindhoven sector had been assigned the longest stretch of the Arnhem road —soon to be christened Hell's Highway. Meeting little opposition, Taylor's units formed up and seized their objectives one after another. However, as they approached the bridge over the Wilhelmina Canal at Zon, a few miles north of Eindhoven, they were pinned down by the accurate fire of a pair of German 88-mm guns in a nearby forest. The 88's were finally destroyed by bazooka fire, but the delay was costly. As the paratroopers tried to rush the Zon bridge, it was blown up in their faces.

Farther up Hell's Highway Jim Gavin's 82nd Airborne was also finding both success and frustration. The 82nd's assault on the long, nine-span bridge over the Maas River at Grave was the most neatly executed strike of the day. Paratroopers landed close to both ends of the bridge. Using irrigation ditches as cover from the fire of a flak tower guarding the bridge, Gavin's men worked their way to within bazooka range. Two rounds silenced the flak tower, and they rushed the bridge and cut the demolition wires. A second key bridge, over the Maas-Waal Canal, was taken in much the same manner. Gavin's two regiments that dropped astride the dominating heights of Groesbeek Ridge southeast of Nijmegen dug themselves in securely on the wooded slopes.

The frustration came at 8 P.M. when, with the division's three primary objectives in the bag, a battalion of the 508th Regiment under Lieutenant Colonel Shields Warren made a dash into Nijmegen to try for the big highway bridge across the Waal. It ran head-on into a newly arrived battalion of the 9th SS Panzer Division. There was a sharp clash in the growing darkness. Warren's men gained the building housing the controls for the demolition charges on the bridge, but the superior firepower of the Panzers drove them away from the span itself.

The Red Devils of the 1st British Airborne executed an almost perfect drop at Arnhem on D-day. It was here, however, that a serious tactical error on the part of Market-Garden's planners caught up with them. The drop zones were six to eight miles west of the city. The need to hold the drop zones for later reinforcements— there were too few aircraft to deliver the full strength of any of the divisions in the D-day lift—meant that General Urquhart could spare but a single battalion to go after the bridge in Arnhem.

That evening five hundred men under Colonel John Frost slipped into the city along an unguarded road and seized the north end of the bridge. At almost the same moment that the 9th SS Panzer was halting Gavin's bid for the Nijmegen bridge, another unit of the same division arrived in time to prevent Frost's men from crossing the Arnhem bridge and taking its southern approach. A second battalion sent to aid Frost was cut off by the Germans on the outskirts of Arnhem.

All in all, the airborne situation at the end of D-day was reasonably satisfactory. Montgomery's red carpet was twenty thousand men strong. The landings had been unexpectedly easy, the easiest in fact that any of the divisions had ever made, in combat or in training. Except for the blown bridge at Zon and the failure of Gavin's coup de main at the Nijmegen bridge, all objectives had been taken or, as at Arnhem, at least denied to the enemy.

The progress of the ground forces was less satisfactory, for the German crust beyond the Meuse-Escaut Canal was thicker and tougher than Allied intelligence had predicted. General Horrocks was forced by the marshy terrain to attack on the narrowest of fronts—the forty-foot width of Hell's Highway. His armor was immediately in trouble. Concealed antitank guns knocked out eight of the Guards Armoured's tanks in rapid succession. Infantry finally flushed the enemy from the woods on the flanks, but it was slow work.

Supported by rocket-firing Typhoon fighter bombers, the Guards battered their way forward, greeted in every village by the cheering Dutch. Portraits of Princess Juliana appeared magically in shop windows. But by nightfall the armored column was still a half dozen miles short of Eindhoven and a linkup with the 101st Airborne.

Heavy rain fell during the night, and in the morning of D-day plus 1—Monday, September 18—there were thick clouds over the Continent and fog over the Allied airfields in England, delaying the second day's lift of glider infantry and supplies. By noon the 101st's paratroopers had liberated Eindhoven, but not until seven that evening did the Guards Armoured link up with them. British engineers went to work building a prefabricated Bailey bridge to replace the blown canal bridge at Zon.

Model and Student began to put in counterattacks. Soon the two American divisions were embroiled in what Max Taylor characterized as "Indian fighting." The fourteen thousand U.S. paratroopers had to control over forty miles of Hell's Highway, which meant a constant scurrying from one threatened sector to another. An example was the fight for the big bridge at Nijmegen. This span was fast becoming the key to the whole Market-Garden operation, and both sides knew it.

The bridge across the Waal in Nijmegen was well over a mile long, with a high, arching center span. Five streets cut through a heavily built-up section of the city to converge on a traffic circle near the bridge's southern entrance. Between the traffic circle and the bridge was a large wooded common known as Hunner Park, where elements of the 9th and 10th SS Panzer divisions had dug in automatic weapons, mortars, self-propelled guns, and at least one of the deadly 88's. Their fire was directed from a massive stone tower in the center of the park.

Just after dawn 82nd Division paratroopers deployed for their second attack on the bridge. The heavy-caliber German fire quickly drove them from the streets. Advancing through alleys and from doorway to doorway, the Americans worked their way to within a block of the traffic circle. That was as far as they got: reinforcements slated for the bridge attack had to turn back to meet a German thrust threatening to overrun the landing zones south of the city where gliders carrying Gavin's artillery battalions were scheduled to land at any minute. The thrust was beaten off and the gliders landed safely—but the Nijmegen bridge remained in German hands.

A planned night attack on Hunner Park was cancelled by General Browning, who was disturbed by reports of a German buildup in front of Groesbeek Ridge to the southeast. If the Germans ever drove the thin line of paratroopers from the ridge, their guns would control both the Maas and Waal bridges, ending any chance of Market-Garden's success.

Colonel Frost's British troopers continued to cling to the north end of the Arnhem bridge, but the enemy repulsed every effort to reinforce the tiny bridgehead. The rest of the Red Devils were besieged at their landing zones west of the city. Communications had completely broken down. The first news from Arnhem was a clandestine telephone call placed by the Dutch underground. Recorded in an 82nd Division intelligence journal, the message was brief and blunt: "Dutch report Germans winning over British at Arnhem."

The chief topic of conversation on the third day of battle, Tuesday, September 19, was the weather. A glider pilot complained of fog so thick that he could see "only three feet of towrope" in front of him. Less than two thirds of the reinforcements and supplies due the 101st arrived, and only a quarter of the 82nd's. A resupply effort at Arnhem was a disaster. Model's troops had finally driven the Red Devils from the drop zones, and a glider pilot on the ground watched in anguish as the C-47's came in and the flak caught them. "They were so helpless! I have never seen anything to illustrate the word 'helpless' more horribly," he recalled. Over 90 per cent of the parachuted supplies fell into enemy hands.

As viewed by a Red Devil in the rear ranks, the situation at Arnhem "was a bloody shambles." The bad weather scrubbed the scheduled drop of the Polish bri-

gade at the south end of the bridge. Every effort to break through to Colonel Frost's battalion failed. Toward evening, in the rain, several German Tiger tanks approached the British bridgehead. To Frost the Tigers looked "like some prehistoric monsters as their great guns swung from side to side breathing flame. . . . We drove these monsters back, but . . . as we prepared for yet another night Arnhem was burning."

Guards Armoured tanks made good progress during the day, jumping off from the new Bailey bridge at Zon at dawn, linking up with Gavin's 82nd Airborne, and reaching the outskirts of Nijmegen by early afternoon. Horrocks met with Gavin and Browning to work out a combined assault on the Nijmegen bridge. Time was a critical factor: the ground forces were now more than thirty-three hours behind the operation's schedule.

The third attack on the Nijmegen bridge jumped off at 3 P.M. Gavin could spare only a battalion from his hard-pressed forces on Groesbeek Ridge. The British contributed an infantry company and a tank battalion. A smaller force of paratroopers and tanks moved against a railroad bridge downstream.

This latter column fought its way through Nijmegen's streets to within five hundred yards of the railroad bridge before it was halted by heavy enemy fire. Every effort to advance farther was stymied, and when an 88 knocked out one of the British tanks, the attackers withdrew.

Meanwhile, the battle for Hunner Park guarding the highway bridge reached its crescendo. Horrocks' tanks had little maneuvering room in the narrow streets, and four of them were set ablaze by antitank fire. The German gunners kept the foot soldiers pinned down. In desperation, paratroopers attempted to advance along rooftops and through buildings, knocking out the connecting walls with explosives. But the enemy fire was too heavy and too well directed. As darkness fell, the third assault on the Nijmegen bridge sputtered out.

News from the 101st's sector to the south was ominous. Student was moving up powerful forces to try to cut Hell's Highway behind Horrocks' armored spearhead. In the late afternoon a squadron of Panther tanks broke through to the road and shot up a British truck convoy. General Taylor himself led a pickup force against the interlopers, and with their single antitank gun they knocked out two Panthers and drove off the rest.

That night the *Luftwaffe* made a devastating raid on Allied-held Eindhoven. "Half a dozen trucks carrying shells were hit directly," reported war correspondent Alan Moorehead, "and at once the shells were detonated and began to add a spasmodic stream of horizontal fire to the bombs which were now falling at a steady rhythm every minute. Presently a number of petrol lorries took fire as well. . . . In the morning one saw with wonder how much of bright Eindhoven was in ruins . . ."

On Wednesday, September 20, the Market-Garden planners expected the Second Army's tanks to be rolling toward the Zuider Zee. Instead they were stymied at Nijmegen. The bombing of Eindhoven and the German shelling of Hell's Highway were having their effects. Ammunition and reinforcements were held up, and the assault boats needed for a new attack on the Nijmegen bridge were delayed almost eight hours. While they waited for the boats, the 82nd Airborne and the Guards Armoured whittled away at the bridge defenses and fought off savage enemy attacks on Groesbeek Ridge. Finally, in midafternoon, the assault boats arrived.

Gavin's plan was to force a crossing a mile downstream from the railroad bridge and take the defenders of both the railroad and highway bridges in the rear. A battalion of paratroopers of the 504th Regiment, commanded by Major Julian A. Cook, was picked to make the crossing. In concert with the amphibious attack, Gavin and Horrocks would hurl every man and tank they could lay their hands on against the southern approach to the highway bridge. H-hour was set for 3 P.M.

As the U.S. Army's official historian phrased it, ". . . an assault crossing of the Waal would have been fraught with difficulties even had it not been so hastily contrived." At this point the Waal is four hundred yards wide, with a swift, ten-mile-an-hour current. The assault boats were unprepossessing plywood and canvas craft nineteen feet in length. There were only twenty-six of them. German strength on the northern bank was unknown; in any case, the paratroopers could not count on surprise, for the crossing site was completely exposed to enemy observers.

Fifteen minutes before H-hour, Allied artillery, tanks, and mortars began to batter the German defenders on the north bank, climaxing their barrage with smoke shells. The wind blew the smoke screen to tatters. At precisely 3 P.M. the 260 men of Major Cook's first wave waded into the shallows, hauling and shoving their awkward craft. They scrambled aboard and with paddles flailing pushed out into the deep, swift stream. Then the Germans opened fire.

Mortars, rifles, machine guns, 20-mm cannon, and 88's thrashed the water until it looked (as a paratrooper described it) like "a school of mackerel on the feed." Shrapnel tore through the canvas sides of the boats, knocking paratroopers sprawling. Of the twenty-six craft in the first wave, thirteen made it across.

Stunned by the ordeal, the paratroopers huddled in the lee of the north bank, retching and gasping for breath. But these men were veterans, trained as an elite force, and as they recovered physically they recovered their poise as well. Although unit organization was hopelessly scrambled, they took stock of the situation and began to move against their tormentors with deadly precision.

They raced forward to seize a sunken road, killing or scattering its German defenders and smashing machine-gun positions with grenades. A pickup platoon stormed an ancient Dutch fortress that dominated the shoreline. With this strongpoint silenced, the paratroopers hurried along the roads leading to the rail and highway bridges.

Meanwhile, weary engineers paddled reinforcements across the Waal. Two more of the flimsy assault boats sank under the enemy's guns. By late afternoon, however, after repeated round trips by the eleven surviving craft, the 504th Regiment had two of its battalions ranged in a solid bridgehead on the north bank of the river.

A mile and a half upstream, the Anglo-American attack on Hunner Park was well under way. During the previous night Model had reinforced the bridge defenders with a battle group from the 10th SS Panzer Division, and several 88's were newly dug in along the north bank, sited to fire into the streets converging on Hunner Park. By now, however, the paratroopers had control of the buildings fronting on the park and were pouring a devastating fire down into the German weapons pits from the rooftops. About an hour and a half after the attack began, an all-or-nothing tank-infantry assault was launched. Charging two and three abreast, the British tanks burst into the park, closely followed by paratroopers. The stone observation tower and a heavily wooded piece of high ground were quickly overwhelmed. The defenders of the park began to withdraw.

It was now dusk, and in the dim light and drifting battle smoke an American flag was seen flying high above the north bank of the river. Taking this as a signal that the far end of the highway bridge was secured, five British tanks raced onto the bridge ramp. In fact the flag was flying from the northern end of the railroad bridge downstream, but no matter: paratroopers were just then overrunning the defenses of the highway bridge as well. German bazookamen hiding in the girders knocked out two of the tanks, but the remaining three clattered across the span, shot their way through a barricade, and just after 7 P.M. were greeted by three grinning privates of the 504th Regiment. The great prize was intact in Allied hands at last; as darkness fell, the final stretch of Hell's Highway lay ahead.

However, the situation of the British paratroopers at Arnhem to the north had grown desperate during the day. Attempts to reinforce Colonel Frost's men at the north end of the bridge were broken off; facing an estimated six thousand German troops, Urquhart could do no more than try to retain a bridgehead on the Lower Rhine a half dozen miles to the west of the city with the remnants of his force. That night a grim message from the Red Devils was received by the British Second Army: "Enemy attacking main bridge in strength. Situation critical for slender force. . . . Relief essential. . . ."

Arnhem is only ten miles beyond Nijmegen, but on Thursday, September 21, it might just as well have been ten light years away. The Guards Armoured Division was immobilized in Nijmegen due to shortages of ammunition, gasoline, and replacement tanks. It had virtually no supporting infantry. The 82nd Airborne was stretched near the breaking point containing attacks on its flank. And to the south on Hell's Highway thousands of supply vehicles were enmeshed in a huge traffic jam.

Thus, the fifth day of Operation Market-Garden was frittered away, much to the frustration of the conquerors of the Nijmegen bridge. Only a trickle of tanks and other fighting vehicles crossed the hard-won span; Allied gains beyond Nijmegen were slight. And at Arnhem the last of Colonel Frost's men, out of ammunition, had been routed from their strongholds and forced to surrender. Allied reconnaissance planes reported seeing German armored units and infantry convoys rolling south, headed toward Nijmegen, across the Arnhem bridge.

The road between Nijmegen and Arnhem runs some six feet above the low fields and orchards flanking it, making the British tanks that tried to advance northward on the next day, Friday, September 22, sitting ducks for the enemy gunners. The advance soon foundered at a roadblock in the village of Ressen, seven miles short of Arnhem.

Although the Germans now held the Arnhem bridge in strength, Horrocks believed a crossing of the Lower Rhine might still be possible by building a bridge downstream, where the Red Devils had their slender bridgehead. Horrocks' troops eventually reached the river over back roads late in the day, but it was too late. German forces arrived on the north bank in too much strength

for Horrocks to attempt a bridging operation.

Thirty miles to the south, Student's tanks slashed across Hell's Highway, bringing all traffic to a halt. Continued bad weather made aerial support and resupply impossible. "Waiting and waiting for the Second Army," wrote one of the Red Devils in his diary. "The Second Army was always at the back of our minds. The thought of it made us stand up to anything. . . ."

On Saturday the Second Army refused to release the reserve division scheduled to be airlifted to the support of the Arnhem airhead. It is an old military maxim to reinforce success, but with each passing hour Market-Garden was looking less and less like a success. Paratroopers of the 101st Division and British tanks managed to reopen Hell's Highway by afternoon, but not enough assault boats could be brought forward to the Lower Rhine to effectively reinforce Urquhart's shrinking perimeter. The Red Devils were critically short of ammunition, food, water, and medical supplies; air resupply was all but impossible, although C-47 pilots repeatedly braved the German flak to try it.

On Sunday, as the Allied command groped for a way to save the battle slipping away from them, Urquhart radioed the Second Army: "Must warn you unless physical contact is made with us early 25 September [Monday] consider it unlikely we can hold out long enough." That evening Student's tanks cut Hell's Highway once more.

At 9:30 A.M. on Monday Generals Browning and Horrocks made it official: Market-Garden had failed; the Arnhem airhead would be evacuated. When night fell the Red Devils began to slip away toward the river, boots and equipment muffled in rags, each paratrooper holding on to the belt of the man in front of him. In a pouring rain rescue boats hurried back and forth across the dark

river under the cover of a steady bombardment by Horrocks' guns. Hundreds of wounded had to be left behind.

Only 2,400 of the nine thousand Red Devils who had fought in and around Arnhem were rescued. When there was time for a count, it was found that in the nine days of fighting the 82nd Airborne had lost over 1,400, the 101st over 2,100. Another fifteen hundred men and seventy tanks were lost by Horrocks' ground forces. Close to three hundred Allied planes were downed.

The Arnhem bridge—the last bridge—stayed firmly in German hands. There it would remain for seven months, until the final few weeks of the war.

Operation Market-Garden came tantalizingly close to success—a few hours saved here, a different decision made there, and everything might have been different. The weather was certainly an important factor in the failure, limiting aerial resupply and reinforcements and hampering air support. The decision to drop the Red Devils so far from Arnhem was a costly one. The pace of the Second Army's rear echelons carrying supplies and reinforcements was hardly what Montgomery had in mind when he called for a drive of "the utmost rapidity and violence." Allied intelligence fumbled badly in not taking reports of the presence of the two Panzer divisions more seriously. And there was pure misfortune in Market-Garden's taking place on the very doorsteps of Model and Student, two of the most skilled German generals on the Western Front.

Most of all, however, Market-Garden failed because it was conceived on the assumption that the German army was about to collapse. The Nazis were not as close to the brink as they seemed: to push them over the edge required a far stronger force than Market-Garden was given. "Perhaps," writes the military historian Charles B. MacDonald, "the only real fault of the plan was overambition."

But if it was a failure, it was a gallant one. If boldness, imagination, and sheer raw courage deserve the reward of victory, then victory should have gone to the men of the First Allied Airborne Army. The fighting record of the 1st British Airborne in Arnhem has been justly celebrated as an epic. Yet the exploits of the two American airborne divisions that defended Hell's Highway against all odds and brilliantly won the great bridge at Nijmegen have too often been overlooked. As General Brereton put it: "The 82nd and 101st Divisions . . . accomplished every one of their objectives. . . . In the years to come everyone will remember Arnhem, but no one will remember that two American divisions fought their hearts out in the Dutch canal country and whipped hell out of the Germans."

"I think we might be going a bridge too far," General Browning had warned a week before the airdrop. Unwittingly, he had framed the epitaph of the greatest airborne assault in history.

*Stephen W. Sears is the editorial director of the American Heritage Education Division.*

*The scenes opposite and below were photographed during the cheerful first forty-eight hours of the assault along Hell's Highway.* OPPOSITE: *The paratrooper receiving admiring glances from Dutch civilians at Zon is from the U.S. 101st Division. A half-track crew leading Guards Armoured tanks gets a warm welcome near Eindhoven. Below left is the mile-long span of the Waal River bridge at Nijmegen, a vital key to Operation Market-Garden. Below right, beleaguered British paratroopers fire a mortar at the enemy outside Arnhem.*

U.S. ARMY

U.P.I.

all in one place—hundreds of railroad cars, thousands of hand tools of every kind, huge compressors, rock drills, as many as eighty steam shovels, and more than a hundred locomotives. And once he set it all in motion, he would go striding about the Cut, ordering this change or that and burning up cigars, as someone said, like Grant at The Wilderness.

The men called him Big Smoke. He talked of bringing in Chinese labor, which bothered a number of people, and he wanted to do away with the eight-hour day. He was working about fourteen hours a day himself and saw no reason why the rest shouldn't too. But everyone agreed that he was the right man for the job. His popularity grew steadily. His earth-moving system worked superbly. When he encouraged rivalry among the steam-shovel crews, it worked better still. After the Army took over, Colonel Goethals would say that no Army engineer of the time could have laid it out, and he would keep the same system in operation, pretty much as it was, until the Canal was finished.

Stevens began excavation in Culebra Cut in early 1906, six months after arriving in Panama and about the time Congress was getting around to debating the question of which sort of canal he ought to be building—a sea-level canal or a lock type. (Stevens had already drawn up plans for both.) It was rather late in the game to belabor the matter, and the chief engineer had long since made up his own mind on the subject. Still, it would be June before Congress would vote on it. The final decision voted by the legislators turned out to be the right one, but only by a narrow margin. Again, Stevens played a decisive role.

When he first came to Panama, Stevens had thought he would be building a sea-level canal. He had a mental picture, he said, of a "wide expanse of blue, rippling water and great ships plowing their way through it like the Straits of Magellan, minus the current." Roosevelt had about the same idea, it seemed. All the same he had appointed a board of distinguished engineers from several countries to consider the problem, and in November, 1905, the board voted 8 to 5 for a sea-level plan. The Navy concurred, John Wallace returned briefly to Washington to contribute his support, and it looked as though a sea-level canal was what almost everyone wanted.

Certainly a sea-level canal had great popular appeal. To the public it appeared that the "Big Ditch" needed only to be dug down deeper to get a canal free of locks, and that whatever extra time and money the job took now would be well spent in the long run. But it was not that simple.

There is, for example, a maximum tidal range on the Pacific side of about twenty feet, but only about twenty inches on the Atlantic side. So even a sea-level canal would require a system of locks to handle the resulting tidal currents. (One sea-level plan called for twin tidal locks a thousand feet long by a hundred feet wide.) In addition, an incredible volume of earth would have to be removed for a sea-level ship channel. In the view of some engineers, including Stevens, the job was beyond what their equipment was up to, and the actual cost would be beyond what the politicians would be willing to pay. The French, it was said, had made that very mistake. De Lesseps had insisted on digging down to sea level even after everyone else had seen it was madness. Their equipment was woefully inadequate, the French engineers had discovered, and by the time de Lesseps (who was not an engineer) gave in and agreed to build a lock canal, it was too late. The French canal company was bankrupt, ridden with corruption, and the whole brave, tragic enterprise collapsed. Stevens' equipment was clearly superior to what the French had, but it was not that much superior—or so argued those who looked on a sea-level canal as decidedly unrealistic.

But the most formidable problem of all was the torrential Chagres River, "the lion in the path" as one authority called it. How it might safely be tamed was a question the sea-level enthusiasts had not resolved. Stevens had had no idea of the volume and violence of the river until he saw it with his own eyes. And in his talks with the other engineers who had been on the Isthmus for some time, he found not a single sea-level man among them—chiefly because of the Chagres. Why Wallace favored the sea-level plan is a puzzle.

But for the others who did (none of whom had had any real experience on the Isthmus), the issue was largely one of building something that would serve the purpose for a long time to come. It was argued that the increasing size of ships would make a lock canal obsolete one day. A sea-level canal would then have to be built to replace it (one of the new canal proposals now being discussed is indeed a sea-level canal), so why not do the job properly in the first place? Besides, as one leading sea-level spokesman pointed out, in all the other great engineering enterprises of the world "there is scarcely a case where the projectors have overshot the mark." Nobody ever seemed to overestimate the needs of the future. It also seemed to the sea-level people that their canal would be less vulnerable to breakdown or to destruction by enemy attack.

After considering the issue firsthand for a while, Stevens became the most powerful and persuasive voice of all for a lock and high-level lake canal. As he saw it, the Isthmus should be bridged by a man-made lake (the largest artificial body of water on earth at the time) with locks at either end stepping down to sea level. The Chagres would supply the lake and the lake would control the Chagres, thereby making a virtue of the Canal's greatest natural obstacle.

It was essentially the same plan as one presented by a brilliant but forgotten French engineer named Adolphe Godin de Lépinay nearly thirty years before, in 1879. Had the French followed the plan, they quite likely would have succeeded. As it was, the plan was still the surest solution beyond question, as Stevens argued with great fervor in his written correspondence with Washington and when he was called back there to testify before a Senate committee.

Stevens made an impressive witness. He explained the increased danger of slides in the construction of a sea-level canal because of the enormous depth of the cut required. Furthermore, he explained, the sea-level canal being talked about would be only 150 feet wide for nearly half its length—a very narrow channel indeed and one that could be blocked for months by a serious slide or collision. When two ships passed in such a channel, one would have to stop and make fast to mooring posts, as at Suez. This procedure, slow and hazardous by day and impossible by night, would drastically reduce the volume of traffic such a canal could handle. A lock canal, on the other hand, would be less expensive to build, less expensive to operate and maintain, and provide faster, safer passage across the Isthmus.

Skillfully, Stevens outlined his plan for an immense earth dam across the Chagres at Gatun, near the Caribbean end of the Canal, which was the key to his whole lock-and-lake scheme. When his description left some of his listeners a little uneasy (the Johnstown flood of 1889 had been caused by the failure of a faulty earth dam), he assured the committee that the earth dam he had designed was quite sound and that such suggested reinforcements as a masonry core would be a superfluous expense.

"Yes, if it is absolutely safe," one senator replied. "Here I suggest that that is a very positive opinion or conviction you have."

"Well, I am a positive man," Stevens answered, and the committee seemed satisfied.

Stevens by this time had also persuaded Roosevelt, originally a sea-level advocate, to formally recommend to Congress that a lock canal be built. It was what the chief engineer wanted, he wrote, and the chief engineer had "a peculiar personal interest in judging aright." Roosevelt by now had taken a great liking to Stevens, called him "a backwoods boy," and admired Stevens' taste for Melville, Poe, and *Huckleberry Finn*.

Through May and June, Stevens lobbied openly on Capitol Hill. He kept to facts and wrote most of what

would be the crucial speech during the Senate debate, which was delivered by the bantam-sized Philander Knox of Pennsylvania—Roosevelt's former trust-busting Attorney General and, interestingly, one of the former owners of the ill-fated dam that caused the Johnstown flood, a fact that escaped attention in 1906.

Knox spoke on June 19. Two days later the Senate voted 36 to 31 for a lock canal. The House soon followed suit. As Navy Captain Miles P. DuVal, Jr., the leading authority on the subject, has written, "This was the great decision in building the Panama Canal." Had the vote gone the other way, had the United States attempted a sea-level canal at that time, the project would have been finished perhaps by 1925 or, more likely, not at all.

Stevens went back to Panama after that, and the work moved ahead at a steady pace. In November, always one of the wettest, unhealthiest months there, Roosevelt arrived. He wanted to see the place at its worst. He spent three historic days sloshing about in tropical downpours, shaking hands, asking innumerable questions, and offering words of inspiration: "You, here, who do your work well in bringing to completion this great enterprise, will stand exactly as the soldiers of a few, and only a few of the most famous armies of all the nations stand in history." Stevens was with him the whole time and stood by while Roosevelt, in a light linen suit, had himself photographed in the driver's seat of a ninety-five-ton steam shovel. The dirt was flying at last.

Exactly what went sour after that is still something of a mystery. Early in 1907, just when all seemed to be going satisfactorily, Stevens, as suddenly as Wallace before him, left the job. On January 30, 1907, he wrote a six-page letter to Roosevelt, who received it less than three months after his return from Panama.

Though there was no formal request for resignation, Stevens clearly wanted out. He complained of "enemies in the rear" and of the discomforts of being "continually subject to attack by a lot of people, and they are not all in private life, that I would not wipe my boots on in the United States." He estimated it was costing him one hundred thousand dollars a year to stay in Panama, considering what he could be earning at home. (He was being paid thirty thousand dollars at the time, an unheard of figure for a government job and the subject of no little carping on the Hill.) The honor of the task appealed to him but slightly, and he could at any time return to positions that "I would prefer to hold, if you will pardon my candor, than the Presidency of the United States."

The work was well in hand and could be completed by men "as competent and far more willing to pick up and carry the burden than I am." Therefore, he concluded, "if in the next two or three months, you can see your way clear to let me follow along other lines much more agreeable to me, I shall ever be your debtor. May I ask your calm and dispassionate consideration of this matter . . ."

Roosevelt's reaction was far from dispassionate. "To say that the President was amazed at the tone and character of the communication is to describe the feelings mildly," wrote one reporter who talked to someone who had been with Roosevelt at the time. The President's first decision had been to put the letter aside until the next morning. Then he sent it over to Taft with a note saying that "Stevens must get out at once." There was a brief meeting, it seems, after which Roosevelt cabled: "STEVENS, PANAMA CANAL: YOUR LETTER RECEIVED AND RESIGNATION ACCEPTED."

It was at this point that Roosevelt decided to turn the whole project over to the Army. At first he appointed Stevens chairman of the Canal Commission, presumably to supervise the military man who would take over the work of construction. But his irritation was evident in his statement, reported by the New York *Tribune*, explaining his choice of a uniformed chief engineer. "Then," he said, "if the man in charge suffers from an enlarged cranium or his nerves go to the bad, I can order him north for his health and fill his place without confusion." The efficient but colorless Goethals, who earlier had accompanied Taft on an inspection tour of the Canal and who was a specialist in locks and dams, was picked immediately for the top command. Stevens declined to remain as chief of the commission, thereby leaving Goethals in full charge.

All kinds of explanations were offered for Stevens' departure. Perhaps he had relied too confidently on Roosevelt's invitation to address him "personally, as man to man, with entire freedom upon any and all matters." There were those who said that he was overworked; that the climate had gotten to him; that the lobbying experience in Washington had turned his stomach; that he had fallen out with the administration over a contract about to be signed with a man who would bring convict labor to Panama.

One intriguing theory offered years later suggested that Stevens had inadvertently stumbled on certain dealings within the administration that, if ever revealed, "would blow up the Republican Party and disclose the most scandalous piece of corruption in the history of the country." The quotation is from Josephus Daniels—later to be Woodrow Wilson's Secretary of the Navy—who also held that the alleged corruption involved the silver-tongued William Nelson Cromwell, the man who had drawn Stevens into the whole Panama affair in the first place.

Stevens refused to discuss the matter. He made no attempt to answer the President's remarks. (The Panama City *Star and Herald*, however, which stood firmly behind Stevens, editorialized that "the top-heavy craniums are located in Washington, and . . . the unsettled nerves are caused by unusual and abnormal political ambitions." And it added that the French were doubtless laughing up their sleeves.) To the men who kept after him for a word of encouragement when the news of his replacement broke, Stevens answered: "Don't talk, dig." A petition was circulated begging him to change his mind. By the time of his leaving, it bore ten thousand signatures.

Stevens officially terminated his service with the Canal at midnight on March 31, 1907. When he sailed away April 8, the crowd that turned out to see him off was like nothing ever witnessed on the Canal before or since. "I have never seen so much affection displayed for any man," wrote Goethals, who had already had to endure a cold reception from Stevens' workmen. As the ship pulled away, Stevens was seen standing at the rail with his son. It was said he looked very pale and sad.

Yet he did not, then or later, break his silence. After the lapse of many years he wrote:

Various reasons for my resignation were given by irresponsible scribblers. They all had points of similarity, as they were all stupid and mendacious. In one respect they were exactly alike; they were all absolutely untrue. I resigned for purely personal reasons, which were in no way, directly or indirectly related to the building of the canal, or with anyone connected with it in any manner.

What these personal reasons may have been he never said or gave even the slightest hint.

He gave up the chance to be immortalized as the builder of the Canal. It was a hard choice to understand. Captain DuVal, who has studied Stevens' Panama career as closely as anyone, believes that Stevens had grown extremely restless, even bored with the job. There may be much to this explanation. Change, Stevens once wrote, was for him among the prime attractions of his profession, and the prospect of another seven years or so at the same thing doubtless had little appeal. He had never remained in one place for very long. Moreover, the creative engineering required had been accomplished and the chief obstacles overcome. The rest would be fairly routine, except for the locks, which were of relatively little interest to him. He really had no desire for personal glory; and once the success of the work was obvious, he was ready to move on, just as he had told Roosevelt he would the first time they met.

The fact that Stevens never adequately explained his decision gives it a certain unavoidable fascination. But apart from that, and the drama of its suddenness, the resignation was really an epilogue. Stevens' real work was over by 1907. Had he stayed on, his further contributions, aside from personal magnetism, would have been relatively few and inconsequential. He also knew comparatively little about hydraulics, which would be the principal concern once the digging was finished and the lock construction started.

Yet Stevens had made extraordinary achievements in remarkably little time. He had created order out of the most disheartening chaos; he had backed Gorgas, without whose efforts the Canal could not have been built—or at least not without an appalling loss of life; he had devised an earth-moving system that did the job; he got the men to care about the work they were doing and established a spirit and a way of life in the Zone that most of them would talk about for the rest of their days; and he successfully championed the lock plan.

One old hand at Panama would later write: "The canal was built in those years [when Stevens was in charge] and from 1907 on nothing would have stopped its being completed." So Stevens, whatever his reasons, had simply walked off stage at that point when there was no longer much left to his part. According to his calculations the work would be completed, the Canal ready to open, on January 1, 1915. He was off by just four and a half months. The first vessel went through on August 15, 1914.

Stevens lived a long and exceedingly active life thereafter. For a time he worked for the New Haven Railroad. Then in the fall of 1909 he went back to work for James J. Hill, secretly, travelling in an open car with his son through the spectacular Deschutes River valley in Oregon and passing himself off as John F. Sampson, a wealthy sportsman interested in trout fishing and possibly buying a little land. His actual purpose was to scout a route for a railroad line southward to San Francisco, which Hill wanted to build—but never did—in direct competition with E. H. Harriman.

Stevens stayed with Hill until 1911, when he set himself up as a consulting engineer in New York. Then, during the First World War, the White House was after him again. In 1917, the year his wife died, Stevens was asked by Woodrow Wilson to go to Russia as head of the American Railway Commission. Stevens, who was sixty-four by that time, accepted and spent the next five years in Russia, Japan, and Manchuria. During the Kerensky regime he directed a reorganization of the vast Trans-Siberian and Chinese Eastern railroads. He was in Russia through the revolution, and as the de facto director (the Russians called him General Stevens) he and some three hundred carefully picked American railroad men kept the Trans-Siberian running through the remainder of the war. After the war, at the request of the Russians, he stayed on as an adviser until 1922.

Stevens lived long enough to see a heroic statue erected in his honor at Marias Pass (in 1925) and to serve as a consultant on the construction of the great Cascades Tunnel, the longest railroad tunnel in America, at Stevens Pass. In 1927 the profession honored him by electing him president of the American Society of Civil Engineers. And in 1937, at the age of eighty-three, he flew off to the Canal in a Pan American clipper. He was immensely impressed by all he saw in Panama and wrote of how clean and healthy the place looked. But the thing that gave him the greatest thrill, he said, was the airplane ride.

His final years were spent in retirement in Southern Pines, North Carolina. He did some advising on a proposed monorail for Los Angeles, was bothered badly by arthritis, and wrote a little about his career. His greatest service to his country, he said, had been to convince Roosevelt and the Congress to build a lock canal. He never said anything to suggest that Goethals' fame as builder of the Canal bothered him the slightest. Goethals, he said, had done a fine job.

Stevens died on June 2, 1943, at the age of ninety. He had outlived Goethals, Taft, Gorgas, Roosevelt—all of them; so he could have had the last word had he chosen.

That Stevens' achievements at Panama had been almost entirely forgotten, even in his own lifetime, was largely his own doing—because he had quit when he did—and doubtless he appreciated this. But Theodore Roosevelt had something to do with this neglect, too.

Roosevelt considered himself a historian as well as a great many other things, and he was so regarded by the public. When Roosevelt came to write about the Canal in his famous *Autobiography*, he never once mentioned the name of John F. Stevens. Gorgas was very briefly credited for his contribution. But the one who "proved to be the man of all others to do the job," according to Roosevelt's version of the story, was Colonel Goethals. Roosevelt said:

It would be impossible to overstate what he has done. It is the greatest task of any kind that any man in the world has accomplished during the years that Colonel Goethals has been at work. It is the greatest task of its own kind that has ever been performed in the world at all.

But Roosevelt's anger at Stevens was not returned in kind. According to Stevens' son, John F. Stevens, Jr., the old engineer, bedridden with his final illness, told him: "Son, the next time you come I shall not be here. On the mantel are the pictures of the only two men who ever influenced my life and I wish you to have them." One of the pictures was of James J. Hill; the other, of Theodore Roosevelt.

*David McCullough, a former editor with this magazine, has written of a dam that failed (*The Johnstown Flood, *Simon & Schuster, 1968) and has a book forthcoming on the Brooklyn Bridge.*

# To The Flag CONTINUED FROM PAGE 75

The pro-"under God" forces received important support in a Lincoln Day sermon the following February. The Reverend George M. Docherty, pastor of the New York Avenue Presbyterian Church, where President Dwight D. Eisenhower worshipped, said, as the President sat in attendance, "There [is] something missing in the pledge, [something that is] . . . the characteristic and definitive factor in the American way of life. Indeed, apart from the mention of the phrase, 'the United States of America,' it could be the pledge of any republic. In fact, I could hear little Muscovites repeat a similar pledge to their hammer-and-sickle flag in Moscow. . . ."

Congress went on to pass a joint resolution adopting the change (apparently no one discovered that the Soviet Union has no such pledge, with or without "under God"), and on Flag Day, June 14, 1954, Eisenhower signed the revision into law. It now read, as it does today:

*I pledge allegiance to the flag of the United States of America and to the republic for which it stands, one nation under God, indivisible, with liberty and justice for all.*

Congressman Rabaut went one step further. He asked songwriter Irving ("Tea for Two") Caesar to set the pledge to music and got the House to authorize the printing of more than three hundred thousand copies of the song. It was sung for the first time in the House chamber on Flag Day, June 14, 1955, by the official Air Force choral group, the Singing Sergeants. Despite a rousing rendition, the tune was quickly forgotten; it had none of the heroic fervor of "The Star-Spangled Banner," which, however unsingable, is a natural for a blood-stirring rendition by band or orchestra. For better or worse, the Pledge of Allegiance will have to make its claim to immortality without benefit of music.

Or perhaps Samuel Butler will prove right in the long run: "Oaths are but words," he said back in 1663, "and words but wind."

# Spoon River Revisited CONTINUED FROM PAGE 17

along with the town during the Depression. He would look out of the window in long silent meditation on the empty square. Then he would say, as much to himself as to me, "I wonder if these towns will ever come back." We both knew they never would.

My Grandfather Laning, who died when I was twelve, was very different—almost as bad a man as Papa Smoot was good. He spent most of his time far away in Oklahoma on his "plantation," and I saw him only on his annual visits to Illinois, when he came back to open the house. He fascinated me, but it was an evil fascination. I was proud of him because he was reputed to be rich, but I always dreaded it a little when he called me to him in the square, because his talk frightened me. I might hear him say to some admiring crony, "When you've got an enemy, don't attack him directly. Put your arm around him—and drive a knife in his back—and twist it!" Once he told me and my companions how, when he was our age, he used to sneak into the Menard House, a tavern that then stood on the south side of the square, to listen to the men's talk. Usually the proprietor ignored him, but sometimes he would chase him away, saying, "Ed, you run along. Abe Lincoln's here, and I don't want you to hear the stories he's got to tell." Sometimes he would invite me to bring my friends up to the house, where he would show us his hunting trophies, the hides and mounted heads of big game he had brought back from his expeditions to the Rocky Mountains, and I would feel very important. By the time I went to high school, I already knew by heart the poem about Grandfather Laning from the *Spoon River Anthology:*

*I have two monuments besides this granite obelisk:*
*One, the house I built on the hill,*
*With its spires, bay windows, and roof of slate;*
*The other, the lake-front in Chicago,*
*Where the railroad keeps a switching yard,*
*With whistling engines and crunching wheels,*
*And smoke and soot thrown over the city,*
*And the crash of cars along the boulevard,—*
*A blot like a hog-pen on the harbor*
*Of a great metropolis, foul as a sty.*
*I helped to give this heritage*
*To generations yet unborn, with my vote*
*In the House of Representatives,*
*And the lure of the thing was to be at rest*
*From the never-ending fright of need,*
*And to give my daughters gentle breeding,*
*And a sense of security in life.*
*But, you see, though I had the mansion house*
*And traveling passes and local distinction,*
*I could hear the whispers, whispers, whispers,*
*Wherever I went, and my daughters grew up*
*With a look as if someone were about to strike them;*
*And they married madly, helter-skelter,*
*Just to get out and have a change.*
*And what was the whole of the business worth?*
*Why, it wasn't worth a damn!*

I was proud of him, but I didn't love him. I loved Papa Smoot.

Though happily married, Mama Smoot harbored some deep dissatisfactions; but I was the only one who knew this. As sometimes happens between grandparents and grandchildren, the difference in age was no barrier between us. Mama liked to go to Springfield, the state capital, twenty miles away, and as soon as I was allowed to drive her car, I would take her there. She would go to Madame Heimlich, the dressmaker, while I went to Barker's Art Store, where there were not only paints and brushes but also a big collection of Civil War books. At the time I was fighting the Civil War all over again— and I was on the side of the Rebellion. Mama Smoot and I would both have such a good time that we were late starting back, and I would have to drive at sixty miles an hour—a fearsome speed for a 1922 Buick over the narrow and unbanked concrete road—in order to get us home ahead of Papa, so that he wouldn't know we had made the trip. On these excursions Mama would tell me that Papa should not have returned to Petersburg from Kansas, where they had gone just after their marriage and where Papa had begun to practice law. If he had stayed in Kansas instead of coming back when his father died, he'd have gone on to become governor. Or he might, if he'd been a little more ambitious, have become senator from Illinois. And he shouldn't have said No when the Chicago & Alton Railroad asked him, after he had helped them obtain their right-of-way through Illinois, to come to Chicago to head their legal department. It was nice to be the first lady of Petersburg and Menard County, but Mama was jealous of Mrs. Potter Palmer. "Papa failed me," she said, "and Harold failed me." (Harold was her only son.) "Now you mustn't fail me." It wasn't enough for her that Papa was the keeper of Petersburg's conscience, state's attorney, and the fundamentalist teacher of the men's Sunday-school class.

Even Papa Smoot betrayed a certain restlessness that seemed to center in me. He would draw me out and argue with me as if it were wicked old Ed Laning, my bad grandfather, the one who hadn't said No to the railroad, that he was sparring with. I did my best in these verbal contests because I knew that the lawyer in him, and the actor, enjoyed the exercise. Uncle Harold would turn white at my temerity, and Mama Smoot would signal her disapproval, but Papa Smoot wouldn't let me off. Once it was Prohibition—the Eighteenth Amendment had just been adopted. I opposed it and he took the defense. He looked angry, but I knew he was pretending. Finally he said to me, "You mean you're not your brother's keeper?" I said of course I wasn't; my brother was a free man and could look out for himself. As soon as I had said it, I knew I had been outwitted. Papa was infinitely pleased with himself—and with me.

I guess they were all restless and dissatisfied, and that's why they sought consolation in moral superiority. Mama defeated herself in this, however. She was an incorrigible gossip, and she poured oil on the flames of Papa's righteous wrath. In the years just before her death she became saintly, and this fault fell away from her; but in her prime she was an awful scourge of sinners. And she always took her discoveries of sin to Papa, and he took them, when he could, to court.

This moral dominion wasn't limited to the poor people who lived down near the tracks in "Joe Town" or over in "Nigger Heaven," or even to the whole town and county, but it extended to people who lived famously and successfully in the great world beyond. When a friend asked my little cousin Dorothy in Kansas City what her grandparents in Illinois were like (Dorothy had just returned from a visit to them), she said, "Mama Smoot writes checks and Papa Smoot walks up and down and spits." And what Papa was spitting about as he paced the floor in the evening might be Mary Pickford and Douglas Fairbanks, who, according to the Chicago *Tribune*, had just married after divorcing their former partners. Papa had never seen a picture show and would as readily have been caught entering Madam Patton's in Springfield as going into a theater. He anathematized the guilty couple and expectorated into the spittoon on the hearth near his big black leather chair.

When the Chicago *Tribune* failed to provide a target for his wrath, there was always Edgar Lee Masters, and in many ways Edgar Lee was even more satisfactory than Mary Pickford, because he was a local boy. Everyone knew him. He had gone to Chicago, where he became a law partner of the successful but infamous Clarence Darrow, who was always defending sinners. And when Edgar Lee came home, it was often in defense of local sinners like the rich merchant whose wife had discovered that he had been carrying on a long love affair with her sister. Edgar Lee himself had recently been divorced. And then he had gone from bad to worse, leaving Darrow's law office to spend all his time writing poetry and leaving Chicago for New York. And on top of everything else—That Damned Book. When *Spoon River Anthology* appeared and won national fame, all hell broke loose. Half the town found itself mirrored there; and all the righteous were condemned, and all the sinners were pardoned. Perhaps the worst of it to Papa Smoot was the poem about Ann Rutledge, especially those lines, "*Beloved in life of Abraham Lincoln,/Wedded to him, not through union,/But through separation.*" This smacked to Papa of some peculiarly horrible moral turpitude which by association he attributed to Edgar Lee. "If that man came to this door and rang the bell, I wouldn't let him in the house!" he would thunder in his courtroom manner, and then he would spit angrily into the spittoon.

This bitterness toward Edgar Lee didn't extend to the poet's Uncle Will, old Billy Masters, or to Aunt Norma, or to their daughter, Miss Edith. Often in the evening after supper, when Uncle Harold and I would take Papa out in the car for his ritual drive, we would stop to pick up Billy, and the two old men would talk, Billy in a high, piping voice that was the relic of an attack of scarlet fever in his youth. Harold would drive first to the C. P. & St.L. station to wait for the 7:15 to go through. At the first faint whistle from the south, Papa would say, "It's Number 49." As the little train rolled past, the conductor would be standing on the back platform to return Papa's and Billy's waves. Then we would speed down Main Street to the crossing a mile away and pull up at the edge of the track, where the conductor would wave just before Number 49 began the long pull up the hill north of town.

Edgar Lee was never mentioned. It would have been morbid to talk of him. Nobody ever did. Sometimes Uncle Harold would ask Billy to tell us about the cyclone that had struck his house out at Sandridge years ago, and Billy would give us a hair-raising account of it. After we had dropped Billy at home, my uncle would assert that Billy hadn't even been there at the time, but Papa Smoot would never take this up. He liked Billy Masters' company better than Harold's. Billy's motto, I would recall, was "Tell a lie never, and the truth not always."

The Masters family, like Lincoln and the Smoots and most of the early settlers of Menard County, had come from Virginia to Kentucky and across Indiana into Illinois, and during the Civil War there were many Copperheads—southern sympathizers—among them. (When he was running for Congress, Lincoln said to his law partner, William H. Herndon, "Next week I'm going back to Menard to make a speech and I'm not looking forward to it. They don't like me back there.") It was years after I had left Petersburg, returning to it only to visit Mama and Papa Smoot, that I came to realize that it was in many ways a southern town. This southern enclave prospered in its isolation until the First World War. The land was fertile and the farmers were rich. Roads were so bad that in winter and spring it was often impossible to make the twenty-mile trip to Springfield. "The Burg" was the busy center of the county's life.

But the war changed everything. When I was eleven, I carried a big flag at the head of the procession that escorted the first group of drafted boys from the courthouse square to the C. & A. depot. Papa Smoot was chairman of the draft board. Down at the Ring Barn, where Ed Shipp's circus had its winter quarters, a little girl in spangled tights sang, "*How're you gonna keep 'em down on the farm, after they've seen Paree?*" A new, flag-waving patriotism swept the country, and this spirit seized upon the image of Lincoln as its symbol. Irving Bacheller, who was writing *A Man for the Ages*, came to Petersburg and

stayed at my friend Hubert's house and strolled through town and over New Salem hill in search of inspiration. A group of "Boosters" led by Judge Nelson, Hubert's father, organized the Lincoln League for the purpose of restoring the village of New Salem, where Abe Lincoln—and Ann Rutledge—had lived. Papa regarded this as foolishness, and the Lincoln League languished for lack of local support.

Ann Rutledge's coffin had been moved from the rural Concord cemetery and brought to the Oakland Cemetery at Petersburg in 1890 (Papa said there wasn't anything in her coffin but a handful of dust and some buttons), and in 1921 the little stone at the head of her new grave, just across the path from Grandfather Laning's granite obelisk, was replaced by a large square block on which was carved Edgar Lee's poem:

*Out of me unworthy and unknown*
*The vibrations of deathless music;*
*"With malice toward none, with charity for all."*
*Out of me the forgiveness of millions toward millions,*
*And the beneficent face of a nation*
*Shining with justice and truth.*
*I am Anne Rutledge who sleep beneath these weeds,*
*Beloved in life of Abraham Lincoln,*
*Wedded to him, not through union,*
*But through separation.*
*Bloom forever, O Republic,*
*From the dust of my bosom!*

I expected a terrible explosion, but none came. Things were changing, even in Petersburg. William Randolph Hearst bought the New Salem hill and gave it to the state of Illinois—on the condition that the state complete the reconstruction of the pioneer village and make it a state park. This development reached the Chicago *Tribune* and the *Tribune* reached Papa Smoot. His reading had become restricted to the Bible and the Chicago *Tribune* (he was, in both cases, a cover-to-cover man), and when I asked him why, he told me, "Everything else is a matter of opinion." The next thing I knew, he was taking visitors to New Salem, and to Oakland Cemetery, too, and he was pointing to these things with pride. And I thought that if Edgar Lee were to come to the door now, Papa would welcome him.

But the explosion did come at last. It came from Edgar Lee. Far away in New York he published a new book, *Lincoln—the Man*. In it he wrote that Lincoln had always been an opportunist politician and that furthermore there had never been any romance between Abe and Ann, that this story was nothing but a fond delusion of Herndon's. ". . . Lincoln had no lasting love, if any love, for Ann Rutledge," he wrote. I thought when I read this that it was no more than we had always known. Uncle Harold had long since told us that Aunt Parthena Nance Hill, the last survivor of New Salem, had often told *him* that while Abe and Ann had known each other, there was certainly no love on either side. But it was awful for Papa Smoot. He got to his feet, with some difficulty now, and he denounced Edgar Lee just the way he used to. "That son of a bitch! If he came to this door and knocked, I wouldn't let him in the house!" And he spat violently into the spittoon.

Papa Smoot's last years were sad, as sad as those of Edgar Lee. The world had broken in and laid waste to Papa Smoot's Petersburg. I couldn't tell him that its heart still beat there in Edgar Lee's room at the Chelsea. While the rest of America advanced under the sign of "Honest Abe" through the years of Harding, Coolidge, and Hoover, Menard County declined. The Depression that was to devastate the whole nation in the early thirties struck the farmers long before. When I came back to visit Papa and drove through the countryside with him and Uncle Harold, he would look out at the unplowed fields and say, "All our troubles come from back there where you are, in New York." And mentally I was looking at another ruined landscape, one described by John Sloan, my teacher (and another resident of the Chelsea). He used to picture for us a ghastly scene in no man's land at night. Over the edge of a shell crater a frightened figure scrambled. It was a banker seeking refuge from the holocaust. Suddenly, by the light of a bursting shell, the banker saw that he was not alone there. Another man sprawled in the dirt and darkness at the bottom of the hole. "Who are you?" demanded the banker. "I'm an artist," the other man said. "I live here." The story comforted me, but I didn't tell it to Papa Smoot.

He welcomed the election of Franklin D. Roosevelt, but as the Depression wore on and he grew old, it seemed to him that the cures prescribed by the government were worse than the disease. "The one thing I hope God will forgive me for when I die," he said, "is that I stumped the county for that man."

Mama Smoot died before Papa, and he didn't want to live any longer after that. I tried to remind him of the consolations of his religion, but the Bible and the Chicago *Tribune* had both lost their efficacy. I don't think Mama and Papa died altogether unfulfilled. I had received some publicity before Mama's death, and she held *Life* magazine before her and said over and over, "And to think that he did it all by himself." And I know that she had persuaded Papa to her point of view once again, because on his deathbed he asked me, "How is your painting going?"—a thing he had never done before.

In 1936 Edgar Lee was invited by the Boosters to make a speech at the celebration of Petersburg's centennial. Miss Edith sent me a copy of his remarks. "No matter where life has taken me," he said, "my heart has remained here. . . . I am one of you. I am prouder that I am sprung from this land than of anything else in my life. I have written books about you, with the idea of

making you beloved where you are not known. My thanks go to you always." He said to them, "The world is upset. . . . In America we are adrift from our old moorings. . . . If anything can save America it will be the Petersburg idea and conception of life, by which I mean self-reliance, courage, integrity, thrift, happiness." Until that last word I'm sure he had his audience with him. If he had said *righteousness* instead . . .

It was not long after this that I began going to see him at the Chelsea. He was a myth of my childhood, an archetype on whom, knowingly and unknowingly, I had modelled myself. He had always lifted Petersburg, for me, to a plane broader and higher than its own view of itself. He had enhanced my life. He told me he had been back home. "I stayed with Uncle Will and Aunt Norma," he said. "I said to them, 'You know how much I've always loved Petersburg. I'm getting old and tired and I'm thinking about coming back and settling down.' Uncle Will piped up, 'Don't you do it! Don't you do it! They'll pluck out every pinfeather you've got!'"

Edgar Lee died in 1950 and was buried in Oakland Cemetery. The Petersburg paper wrote, "Let us not discuss his books or his philosophy or his individualism. Suffice it to say that Edgar Lee Masters has come home."

---

*One of America's most distinguished artists, Edward Laning lives and works in New York and is president of the National Society of Mural Painters. His "Memoirs of a* WPA *Painter" appeared in our October, 1970, issue.*

Oakland Cemetery, Petersburg: "*All, all are sleeping, sleeping, sleeping on the hill.*"

*Mrs. Jones of Walla Walla,*
*Mrs. Smith of Kankakee,*
*Mrs. Cohen, Mrs. Murphy*
*Sing your praises lustily.*

*There's a baby in every bottle,*
*So the old quotation ran,*
*But the Federal Trade Commission*
*Still insists you'll need a man.*

Refrain:  *OH-H-H, we'll sing of Lydia Pinkham*
*And her love for the Human Race.*
*How she sells her Vegetable Compound,*
*And the papers, the papers they publish,*
*they publish her FACE!*

No objections were ever raised by the Pinkham Medicine Company to the free advertising contained in the quips and the sometimes-ribald verses about the efficacy of their product.

Lydia didn't have long to enjoy her success. She died in 1883, but her fame went marching on. For years the *Ladies Home Journal* tried in exasperation to explain to its readers that Lydia had gone to her reward and that when suffering women wrote to her, the reply came from a corps of ten-dollar-a-week clerks. Edward Bok, the editor of the *Journal*, even printed a photograph of Lydia's tombstone. It made no difference. His readers preferred old error to new truth and steadfastly clung to the belief that their medical friend was still slaving away for them in her laboratory in Lynn, Massachusetts. Thousands of sufferers continued to write about their troubles. They took the medicine. They felt better. Who can say flatly that they were absolutely cheated? The Vegetable Compound did, after all, provide the customers with psychological sedation and the geniality of a cocktail.

Many of the secret remedies were, however, cruelly vicious, especially that category containing habit-forming drugs. Dr. Swayme's Wild Cherry Tonic, for example, which "cured" tuberculosis, depended for its analgesic effect upon morphine, "the draught . . . that bids Consumption fly." The usage of opium derivatives, such as codeine or cocaine, was so general during and after the Civil War that addiction was commonly described by the euphemism "the Army disease." Especially insidious were the catarrh powders and the soothing syrups whose content of morphine sulphate made it certain that teething children would not fret. Even more brutal, if one can make a very fine distinction, were the mail-order drug-habit "cures" that followed the "hair of the dog" theory. "Practically all of these advertised

remedies are simply the drug itself in concealed form," wrote Samuel Hopkins Adams in his exposé, *The Great American Fraud* (1906). No wonder, then, that the "Gradual Reduction Treatment" was so gradual that the victims were under treatment for up to twenty years.

The contact between those who were doctoring and the picturesque characters who supplied the necessary merchandise was even more intimate when the medicine-show artists came to town; for example, such a remarkable individual as "Doc," or sometimes "Colonel," John E. Healy. Healy travelled the eastern parts of the United States in a big, brightly painted wagon in the interest of the Healy Liver Pad Concert Company. After a free show by the three performers who made up the cast there was a subtle change of mood. The Doctor-Colonel came forward and gravely began his pitch: "These pads, ladies and gentlemen, contain no harmful chemicals . . ." This was a true statement. According to competing professors the pads were stuffed with sawdust that had been doped to "smell like a drugstore."

Later Healy, in an inspired moment, thought of peddling Indian herb medicines through the Indians themselves, thus capitalizing on curiosity about the Old West. The Indians would arrive in a town like Colebrook, New Hampshire, and set up their tepees with their medicinal herbs bubbling in a pot right in front of the tents. Out of this imaginative concept came the Kickapoo Indian Medicine Company. In its great days this firm sent out from seventy-five to a hundred complete carnival companies in a single season, known as the Kicks in the circus world. Each one was under the guidance of a long-haired "grinder," or "Indian Agent," who gave the medical lecture decked out in a yellow buckskin costume and looking like General Custer in Cassily Adams' gory but fascinating color lithograph, *Custer's Last Fight.*

The scenario for the Kicks, which originally called for cooking up the medicines in front of the wigwams, proved cumbersome. So Healy and his partner, "Texas Charley" Bigelow, settled for having the Indians out on the western plains ship the dry botanicals to New Haven, Connecticut, where they were processed in a factory at 521 Grand Avenue. It was known in company nomenclature as the Principal Wigwam.

There were also skillful women practitioners of tailgate medicine. Among them Madame DuBois should at least be mentioned. She travelled with a brass band and pulled teeth; also Princess Iola, née Eva Billings, of Quincy, Illinois, who pitched complexion soap, which was whatever soap was sold at the local dime store, cut up into small chunks and rewrapped in foil. Another exotic princess, Little Lotus Blossom, was in fact a Min-

*Dr. Rose, unknown to history beyond the fact that his office was on the way to the cemetery, hung a special shingle out whenever a funeral cortege passed by. "Not my patient," it smugly explained. The bottles, now collectors' items, held ginger tonic and cod-liver oil.*

nesota farm girl who lectured on Tiger Fat, a salve, and on Vital Sparks, a remarkable discovery from faraway Outer Mongolia that pepped up aging males who were getting worried about the performance of marital duties. For this charade Lotus Blossom wore a mandarin coat and a little Chinese skull cap. Later she developed a scientific spiel under the name Madame V. Pasteur. The V. was authentic since her name was Violet. Madame never mentioned Louis Pasteur, but she had a cultivated manner, and for this routine she wore an academic cap and gown and referred frequently during her discourse to Ponce de Léon, the bacteriologist Elie Metchnikoff, and the body toxins. In each of her roles Violet followed the stern law of social Darwinism as practiced by such star performers on the gasoline-torch circuit as Prince Nanzetta, Big Foot Bill Wallace, and Hal the Healer: "Take the easy dough and get out of town fast." The guys and dolls who were masters of long con (slow, deliberate persuasion) and short con (snappy, aggressive delivery) are album memories now, retired by burdensome taxes and local regulations, closed towns, and the competition of more sophisticated forms of mass entertainment.

Curiously enough, the advances made in chemistry, technology, and medical research have created vastly increased opportunities for the operations of charlatans, as it has become more difficult for the laity to discriminate between genuine achievements and clever frauds. Whatever is new and interesting to the general public has always provided a topical approach for quackery. Electricity led on to Electric Bitters; the germ theory of disease, to Radam's Microbe Killer. Publicity about the newer knowledge of the glands of internal secretion suggested to the imaginative proprietors of the Capricorn Chemical Company the idea of goat gland tablets.

The serious objection to quack medicines was that they were useless, that they delayed or prevented the patient from getting proper treatment, and, at the worst, that they contained deleterious substances, including narcotics. The effort to establish some federal control in this area dates as far back as 1879. It built up rapidly in the period 1898–1904, and a consumer-protection law, despite bitter opposition from the powerful Proprietary Association, was passed by Congress and signed into law by President Theodore Roosevelt under the name of the

Pure Food and Drug Act of 1906. This was the most significant legislation of the Progressive Era in the field of "consumerism," subsequently strengthened by amendment and legal interpretation and enlarged to cover therapeutic mechanical devices, such as the electric-belt fake, the wire-and-gas-pipe Oxydonor, brain child of Dr. Hercules Sanche, and the magic black box of Dr. Albert Abrams, which gave off a humming sound. Abrams, a licensed physician prominent enough to be listed in *Who's Who in America*, had wandered, alas, down the primrose path of quackery, but he was solaced by the number of tax-free dollars in his bank account.

Some of these gaudy deceivers have left permanent monuments in one form or another. Gaylord Wilshire, who invented a contraption called the I-On-A-Co, a sort of magic horse collar worn around the neck, was one of the great con men of all time and is memorialized in Wilshire Boulevard, in Los Angeles. And Dr. J. C. Ayer, an astute businessman who channelled his hair-restorer and cherry-pectoral money into paper and cotton mills, had a town, Ayer, Massachusetts, named after him. Specimens of the gadgets that flashed lights and made interesting noises still exist, as memorials to the fool who could not be saved from his folly, in the collections of the Smithsonian Institution, the American Medical Association, the California Department of Public Health, and the Armed Forces Institute of Pathology. Each exhibit testifies to the selling power of pseudoscientific jargon.

The masters of medical humbug have been inconvenienced but not eliminated by the authority that has been confided to various governmental agencies: the Federal Trade Commission, the Food and Drug Administration, and the Post Office Department. A few years ago we saw the spectacular rise, and fortunately the steep decline, of Dudley Joseph LeBlanc's Hadacol. Hadacol consisted of vitamins, minerals, honey, and firewater and was brilliantly promoted by the old, reliable medical con methods. There was a moment of truth, mingled with levity, when Groucho Marx once asked LeBlanc on a television program what Hadacol was good for. Its pappy replied in a flash of misunderstanding, "Hadacol was good for five million dollars last year."

Grandfather was a mark, and no mistake about it

(*mark.* Synonyms: rube, chump, simp, goof, gill). Yet the take in violation of federal laws even today is around one billion dollars a year, and the depredations of medical banditry get less amusing as they come closer to us.

"If we add to this billion dollars the direct costs of local quackery and the indirect costs of health misinformation," says Wallace F. Janssen, historian of the Food and Drug Administration, "I believe a total figure of $2 billion represents a conservative estimate. The costs in terms of human values are, of course, beyond computing."

Door-to-door pill peddlers, often little old ladies in sneakers, still ply their folksy trade ("We're not doctors, see? But if you want to get rid of that lump in your breast for only seventeen dollars a month . . ."). Worthless diagnostic machines proliferate for the treatment of exophthalmic goiter, or what have you. It took the Federal Trade Commission sixteen years, one hundred and forty-nine hearing sessions, eleven thousand pages of testimony, more than a million dollars, and a trip to the Supreme Court to eliminate the little word *liver* from the trade name and advertising of Carter's Little Liver Pills. But it was legally determined, at long last, that the seventy-year-old preparation, a laxative, did not have any perceptible effect upon the liver.

A similar battle, with the outcome still in doubt, now rages between the government forces and the makers of Geritol, a vitamin proposition that for eleven years has defied the orders of the Federal Trade Commission to cease and desist from claiming that there is a widespread pathological condition known to medical science as Tired Blood. Geritol comes to the rescue with "iron power," provided that one has iron deficiency, which is highly unlikely.

How does Geritol go about enriching the hemoglobin, putting the old moxie back into your blood cells, right from the first spoonful?

Well, you see . . .

---

*Gerald Carson, an engaging social historian who is a frequent contributor, has covered various alcoholic subjects for* AMERICAN HERITAGE—*saloons and the whiskey tax, for instance. The story of "patent" medicines like Lydia Pinkham's original 35.8 proof Vegetable Compound is a natural offshoot of this interest.*

# POSTSCRIPTS TO HISTORY

## WORKS IN PROGRESS

A restorer was already busy trying to save the Ben Shahn mural in the Bronx Central Post Office in New York City when the article in which it was featured, Edward Laning's "Memoirs of a WPA Painter," appeared in our October, 1970, issue. According to the General Services Administration, the restoration was more complex than was anticipated because of the "strange reaction of the plaster on the tempera, aided by the accumulation of 30 years of dirt." In addition, Karel Yasko, special assistant to the commissioner, Public Buildings Service, G.S.A., had this welcome news to report:

Our next salvation is directed at the Edward Laning murals on Ellis Island. This *is* a direct result of your story. I had been informed previously that they had deteriorated beyond recall but when your photograph indicated that at least one was seemingly intact, we felt compelled to try to save it. . . .

Mr. Yasko also reports that an inventory has been started to locate all works of art that were commissioned by the federal government and are still in its possession, especially those done between 1933 and 1943. Perhaps a full-scale restoration policy will result.

## SIC TRANSIT

Considering the toil, time, and hardship it took to build the Panama Canal (see page 64), it seems almost flippant to report that a three-foot-long model cruiser named *Ancon* II last year became the smallest vessel ever to pass through the Canal. The boat, built from a kit by Major Kenneth Thomas of the U.S. Air Force, made the journey from the Atlantic side to the Pacific in eight and a half hours. *Ancon* II carried two and a half gallons of fuel for her nine-tenths-of-a-horsepower engine. She could reach nine knots when fully loaded, twelve knots as she became lighter. The boat was guided by a radio transmitter and was lifted from one level to another through the locks by being tied to a control boat, aboard which was a Canal pilot. Major Thomas paid seventy-two cents for the fifty-mile transit, the minimum rate for a ship in ballast.

## AUTHOR PENS HISTORIC HEADS

Gerald Carson, a frequent contributor to this magazine (see "Sweet Extract of Hokum" on page 18 of this issue), dropped us a note after perusing the headlines about newsworthy occurrences that appeared in our February issue ("Through History With the *Times*"). Herewith his remarks:

To amuse myself while suffering a winter cold, I tried your AMERICAN HERITAGE headline game; of course, it is really the *New York Times* headline game too, but I very much enjoyed your collection of world events as that august and restrained newspaper might have covered them if it had existed far back in history. I enclose four candidates:

> CLEOPATRA MAPS BARGE WEDDING
> NAB GUY FAWKES IN CELLAR PLOT
> YALE MAN HANGS FOR ROLE AS SPY
> ROME TO FEATURE BREAD, CIRCUSES

## NEW NAME, SAME PERSON

For the first time, the signature that appears on greenbacks has been changed while the Treasurer of the United States is still in office. New paper currency is now signed Dorothy Andrews Kabis instead of Dorothy Andrews Elston, a result of the Treasurer's marriage last September to W. L. Kabis.

## A SCHOOLED INDIAN

Our article on the Carlisle Indian School ("The Great White Father's Little Red Indian School," December, 1970) questioned the wisdom and results of trying to "civilize" the red man. One graduate who apparently remained close to the old ways, at least outwardly, was the gentleman pictured below. His photograph was supplied by Robert A. Murdock, executive director of the Association for the Preservation of Virginia Antiquities, in Richmond. Mr. Murdock reports that the picture was taken by his wife's great uncle, Jack Harrah of Montana, in 1934. The inscription on the back says: "Flathead Chief—'Sam Resurection.' Has fine home but lives in tepee back of house. 90 years old. Personal friend & guide for Teddy Roosevelt in all his hunting trips in U.S. Graduate of Carlyle College."

As Mr. Murdock observed, "If accurate the inscription : . . reveals the inability of Carlisle to completely transform all of its students."

For another look at the American Indian, in the years immediately after the high point of his resistance to white incursions, see pages 40–41 of this issue.

*Sam Resurection*

# THE REVISIONIST: *Lexington, 1775*

DRAWN BY MICHAEL RAMUS